School Quiz Book

by
Saurabh Aggarwal

Published by:

F-2/16, Ansari Road, Daryaganj, New Delhi-110002
011-23240026, 011-23240027 • *Fax* 011-23240028
Email info@vspublishers.com • *Website* www.vspublishers.com

Regional Office Hyderabad
5-1-707/1, Brij Bhawan (Beside Central Bank of India Lane)
Bank Street, Koti, Hyderabad - 500 095
040-24737290
E-mail vspublishershyd@gmail.com

Branch Office Mumbai
Godown # 34 at The Model Co-Operative Housing, Society Ltd.,
"Sahakar Niwas", Ground Floor, Next to Sobo Central, Mumbai - 400 034
022-23510736
E-mail vspublishersmum@gmail.com

Follow us on:

All books available at **www.vspublishers.com**

© Copyright : Author
ISBN 978-93-505716-8-2
Edition 2014

The Copyright of this book, as well as all matter contained herein (including illustrations) rests with the Publisher. No person shall copy the name of the book, its title design, matter and illustrations in any form and in any language, totally or partially or in any form. Anybody doing so shall face legal action and will be responsible for damages.

Printed at : Param Offseters Okhla New Delhi-110020

Publisher's Note

V&S Publishers, after publishing a number of Quiz Books, such as the *Business Quiz Book, Environment Quiz Book, Quiz Time History, Quiz Time Mathematics*, etc., are now coming up with this altogether new and exclusive book for **school children, especially in the age group of 10 to 18 years** called the *School Quiz Book.* The book contains questions in different sections in the form of Fill in the Blanks, Crosswords, Facts, Multiple Choice Questions, etc., on a number of subjects, like General Knowledge, Science, Geography, History, Political Science, Current Affairs, etc.

The main purpose of publishing this book is to give a complete, updated and comprehensive knowledge of all the above mentioned subjects; a good metal exercise for students, who are opting for various competitive examinations and also to enhance the IQ of the school kids in general, particularly those of the Middle, Secondary and the Senior Secondary School levels.

Moreover, nowadays, there is so much competition that to get admission in good schools and colleges, one has to go through several entrance tests and interviews which require a student to be well-equipped in General Knowledge, Current Affairs and have an in depth knowledge of Science, Geography, History, Mathematics, etc. The ***School Quiz Book*** has been aimed to solve this purpose effectively, as all the sections containing different types of questions have been followed with their respective answers to help the students self-evaluate themselves.

Hence dear readers, the book is a 'must read' for all, particularly for the schoolchildren from classes 6th to 12th standards.

Contents

Publisher's Note	3
Who am I?	7
Identify the Pictures	17
Complete the Sentences with Appropriate Words	62
CROSSWORD - 1	88
CROSSWORD - 2	90
CROSSWORD - 3	92
CROSSWORD - 4	94
CROSSWORD - 5	96
CROSSWORD - 6	98
CROSSWORD - 7	100
CROSSWORD - 8	102
CROSSWORD - 9	104
CROSSWORD - 10	106
CROSSWORD - 1	108
CROSSWORD - 2	108
CROSSWORD - 3	109
CROSSWORD - 4	109
CROSSWORD - 5	110
CROSSWORD - 6	110
CROSSWORD - 7	111
CROSSWORD - 8	111
CROSSWORD - 9	112
CROSSWORD - 10	113
Multiple Choice Questions	114

Who am I?

Question 1

1. I was a Member of Parliament (MP) in the United Kingdom House of Commons between 1892 and 1895, and the first Asian to be a British MP. My book, *Poverty and Un-British Rule in India* brought attention to the draining of India's wealth into Britain.
2. I am credited with the founding of the *Indian National Congress*, along with *A.O. Hume*.
3. I am known as the *Grand Old Man of India*.

Question 2

1. I was born as Narendranath Datta.
2. I am perhaps best known for my inspiring speech which began, "Sisters and brothers of America ...," in which I introduced Hinduism at the *Parliament of the World's Religions in Chicago in 1893*.
3. I was the chief disciple of the 19th-century saint Ramakrishna. I founded the *Ramakrishna Math* and the *Ramakrishna Mission*.

Question 3

1. I was born as Cassius Marcellus Clay, Jr. in 1942.
2. In 1967, I refused to be conscripted into the U.S. military, citing my religious beliefs and opposition to the Vietnam War. I was eventually arrested and found guilty on draft evasion

charges and stripped off my boxing title.

3. Nicknamed 'The Greatest', I was involved in several historic boxing matches.

Question 4

1. I am remembered for killing a fully grown tiger with his bare hands in a jungle of Bihar.
2. I extended the Grand Trunk Road from Chittagong in Bangladesh to Kabul in Afghanistan.
3. During my five-year-rule from 1540 to 1545, I set up a new civic and military administration, issued the first Rupee and re-organised the Postal System of India.

Question 5

1. I was born in the United Kingdom and first worked as a chemist before becoming a lawyer.
2. I am famous for my 'iron resolve'.
3. I am the first woman to hold the post of the Prime Minister in my country of birth.

Question 6

1. I was born as Anjezë Gonxhe Bojaxhiu on August 26, 1910.
2. I am the recipient of numerous honours including the *1979 Nobel Peace Prize*.
3. One of my famous quotes is: "By blood, I am Albanian. By citizenship, an Indian. By faith, I am a Catholic nun. As to my calling, I belong to the world. As to my heart, I belong entirely to the Heart of Jesus."

Question 7

1. I was named after the town of my birth.
2. I am the founder of *modern nursing*. The pledge taken by new

| Who am I? | | 9 |

nurses was named in my honour, and the annual *International Nurses Day* is celebrated around the world on my birthday.
3. I was dubbed, 'The Lady with the Lamp' after my habit of making rounds at night.

Question 8

1. In 1919, I co-founded the distribution company, United Artists, giving me a complete control over my films.
2. I became a worldwide icon through my screen persona, 'The Tramp'.
3. I was an English comic actor and filmmaker, who rose to fame in the silent era.

Question 9

1. According to *The Mahabharata,* my name means, 'the horse-voiced'.
2. I am the grandson of the Brahmin sage, Bharadwaja. I fought on the Kaurava side against the Pandavas in the Mahabharata war.
3. The rumours about my death in the Kurukshetra war led to the death of Drona at the hands of Prince Dhrishtadyumna.

Question 10

1. When India became independent in 1947, I represented India at the UNESCO (1946–52) and was later the *Ambassador of India to the Soviet Union*, from 1949 to 1952.
2. In 1939, Pt. Madan Mohan Malaviya invited me to succeed him as the Vice-Chancellor of the Banaras Hindu University (BHU). I served as its *Vice-Chancellor* till January 1948.
3. I believed that "teachers should be the best minds in the country."

Question 11

1. In the 1960 film, *Mughal-e-Azam*, I was portrayed by Dilip Kumar.
2. I was born as Nur-ud-din Mohammad Salim.
3. Mehr-un-Nissa, Empress of the Mughal Empire was my chief consort.

Question 12

1. My body was originally buried in St. Francis church, Kochi.
2. I was named in 1524 as the Governor of India, under the title of Viceroy, and given the newly created County of Vidigueira in 1519.
3. I am one of the most famous and celebrated explorers from the Discovery Ages, being the first European to reach India by the sea.

Question 13

1. I was recruited around 1899 by George Eastman to serve as the vice-chairman of the board of the British company, Kodak Limited, affiliated with the *Eastman Kodak*.
2. It is believed that 'PNP' in my signature stands for 'Professor of Natural Philosophy.'
3. I am widely known for determining the correct value of absolute zero as approximately -273.15 Degree Celsius.

Question 14

1. I was awarded the *first Nobel Prize in Physics* in 1901.
2. In the honour of my accomplishments, the International Union of Pure and Applied Chemistry (IUPAC) named element 111, a very radioactive element with multiple unstable isotopes, after me.

Who am I?		11

3. Nearly two weeks after my discovery, I took the very first picture using X-rays of my wife, Anna Bertha's hand. When she saw her skeleton she exclaimed, "I have seen my death!"

Question 15

1. Mycroft is my elder brother. I made my first appearance in *Beeton's Christmas Annual* in 1887.
2. I was inspired by Dr. Joseph Bell, for whom my creator had worked as a clerk at the *Royal Infirmary of Edinburgh*.
3. I was created by the Scottish author and physician, Sir Arthur Conan Doyle.

Question 16

1. I was born as Dhanpat Rai Srivastava.
2. I began writing under the pen name, 'NawabRai'.
3. In my last days, I focussed on village life as a stage for complex drama, as seen in the novel, *Godan* and the short-story collection, *Kafan*.

Question 17

1. I was the co-founder of Jamia Milia Islamia, serving as its Vice Chancellor from 1928.
2. I died on May 3, 1969, the first Indian President to die in office.
3. I was the country's first Muslim President.

Question 18

1. I was visiting the United States when Adolf Hitler came to power in 1933 and I did not go back to Germany, where I had been a professor at the Berlin Academy of Sciences. I settled in the U.S., becoming an American citizen in 1940.
2. I am a favourite model for depictions of mad scientists and absent-minded professors; my expressive face and distinctive

hairstyle has been widely copied and exaggerated.
3. I received the *1921 Nobel Prize in Physics* 'for my services to theoretical physics, and especially for my discovery of the law of the photoelectric effect'.

Question 19

1. I was born as Arjumand Banu Begum in Agra into a family of Persian nobility, as a daughter of Abdul Hasan Asaf Khan.
2. A UNESCO World Heritage Site in India was constructed by my husband as my final resting place.
3. I mothered fourteen children including Aurangzeb, the son who temporarily succeeded my husband until deposed by his brother.

Question 20

1. A revivalist for Buddhism in India, I inspired the *Modernist Buddhist Movement* in *Maharashtra* which was spreading all across India and was also called the *Dalit Buddhist Movement*.
2. The *Reserve Bank of India (RBI)*, formed in 1934, was based on the ideas that I presented to the *Hilton Young Commission*.
3. As independent India's first law minister, I was the principal architect of the Constitution of India.

Question 21

1. I am a fictional character created by *Elzie Crisler Segar*.
2. I have an *anchor tattoo*, one on each arm.
3. In honour of my 75th anniversary, the Empire State Building illuminated its notable tower lights green in the weekend of January 16–18, 2004 as a tribute towards my love of 'spinach'.

Question 22

1. I was renamed *Jalal-ud-din Muhammad* by *Humayun*, a name which he had heard in his dream at Lahore.

2. The *Mansabdari system* was instituted by me. It was the generic term for the military-type grading of all imperial officials of the Mughal Empire.
3. *Dīn-i Ilāhī* was a religion propounded by me.

Question 23

1. One of my famous phrases is "Math class is tough!"
2. I was created by American businesswoman, Ruth Handler. My name is inspired by my founder's daughter, Barbara.
3. I am a fashion doll manufactured by the American toy-company, Mattel, Inc.

Question 24

1. I founded the *Swatantra Party* and was one of the first recipients of India's highest civilian award, the *Bharat Ratna*.
2. During my lifetime, I acquired the nickname, *'Mango of Salem'*. Supported by Jawaharlal Nehru, I was appointed the *first Governor of West Bengal*.
3. I was the *last Governor-General* of India.

Question 25

1. The British colonial authorities called me, *'Father of the Indian unrest.'* I am the author of the book, *The Arctic Home in the Vedas*.
2. I started the Marathi weekly, *Kesari* in 1880-81 with *Gopal Ganesh Agarkar as the first editor*.
3. I was conferred with the honorary title of 'Lokmanya', which literally means, "Accepted by the people (as their leader)".

Question 26

1. I was the music director of the *All India Radio, New Delhi*, from 1949 to 1956.

2. I had an affair with Sue Jones, a New York concert producer, which resulted in the birth of Norah Jones in 1979.
3. I gave up dancing in 1938 to study sitar playing under the court musician, Allauddin Khan.

Question 27

1. Pandit Jawaharlal Nehru had the following to say about me, "Who am I, a mere Prime Minister before a Queen, a *Queen of Music*."
2. My first movie, *Sevasadanam* was released on May 2, 1938.
3. I am the first musician ever to be awarded the *Bharat Ratna* and I am the first Indian musician to receive the *Ramon Magsaysay award*.

Question 28

1. I am dedicated to the Prisoners of Ahmednagar jail. I chronicled the history of India beginning from the Indus Valley Civilization, and then covered the country's history from the arrival of the Aryans to the government under the British Empire.
2. I am the basis of the 53-episode Indian television series, *Bharat Ek Khoj* (1988), directed by Shyam Benegal.
3. I was written by India's first Prime Minister.

Question 29

1. In 1896, I wrote *Niruddesher Kahini*, the first major work in Bengali science fiction.
2. My residence 'Acharya Bhavan', built in 1902, has been turned into a museum.
3. *Crescograph, a device for measuring growth in plants*, was invented by me in the early 20th century. I pioneered the *investigation of radio* and *microwave optics*.

| Who am I? | ? | 15 |

Question 30

1. I am the first Indian monument to have an e-ticket facility.
2. My construction started in 1192 by Qutub-ud-din Aibak and was completed by Iltutmish.
3. I have *379 stairs*, a height of *72.5 metres (237.8 ft)*, and have a base *diameter of 14.3 metres*, which narrows to *2.7 metres at the top storey*.

Answers

1. Dadabhai Naoroji
2. Swami Vivekananda
3. Muhammad Ali
4. Sher Shah Suri
5. Margaret Thatcher
6. Mother Teresa
7. Florence Nightingale
8. Charlie Chaplin
9. Ashwatthama
10. Dr. Sarvepalli Radhakrishnan
11. Jahangir
12. Vasco da Gama
13. Lord Kelvin
14. Wilhelm Röentgen
15. Sherlock Holmes
16. Munshi Premchand
17. Dr. Zakir Hussain
18. Albert Einstein
19. Mumtaz Mahal
20. Bhimrao Ramji Ambedkar
21. Popeye
22. Akbar
23. Barbie
24. C. Rajagopalachari
25. Bal Gangadhar Tilak
26. Ravi Shankar
27. M.S. Subbulakshmi
28. Discovery of India
29. Sir Jagadish Chandra Bose
30. Qutub Minar

Identify the Pictures

1. *Orville* and *Wilbur* operated a *bicycle repair shop* in *Dayton, Ohio*, before creating their most successful invention. How do we popularly know them?

2. Identify the lab equipment.

   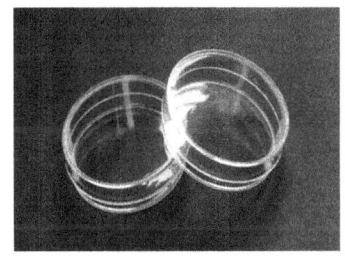

3. In which industry would you find the converter shown below?

   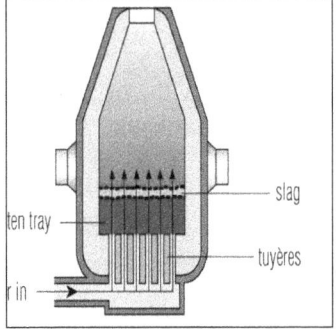

4. Identify the revolutionary.

5. Identify the Vishnu *avatar*.

6. Identify the instrument in Narada's hand.

Identify the Pictures

7. She was the only Indian woman to become the President of the United Nations General Assembly. Identify her.

8. Identify the form of painting.

9. He is known as the *father of Indian cinema* and a popular award is named after him. Who is he?

10. Identify the founder of the Mauryan empire.

11. In which Indian state is the following monument located?

12. He was the court jester of which emperor of the Vijayanagara Empire in the 16th century?

Identify the Pictures

13. The following dance form originated in which state during the 17th century and has developed over the years with improved looks, refined gestures and added themes besides more ornate singing and precise drumming?

14. Identify the famous temple of Lord Shiva situated in Nepal.

15. An Indian freedom fighter and politician in Uttar Pradesh, she became the first woman to be elected the Chief Minister of Uttar Pradesh. Identify her.

16. Name the famous chess Grandmaster.

17. Identify the words written below this logo.

18. In which city would you find this skyscraper?

Identify the Pictures

19. Can you name this gaming console?

20. Identify the sports personality. He was the subject of a recent Bollywood movie.

21. Name the species. This family is the largest family of flowering plants.

22. In which city would you find this?

23. Identify the Indian nobel laureate.

24. Identify the unique structure given below.

Identify the Pictures

25. Identify the adventure sport.

26. Identify the 35th President of the United States, serving from 1961 until his death in 1963.

27. Name the host of the Indian version of this television series.

28. Identify the Indian city where you find a temple of these three Gods and Goddesses.

29. With the distinctive honour of being India's first pilot, he was instrumental in giving wings to what is now known as *Air India*. Who is the person described and shown in the picture?

30. Who designed this flying machine, which did not produce any concrete results?

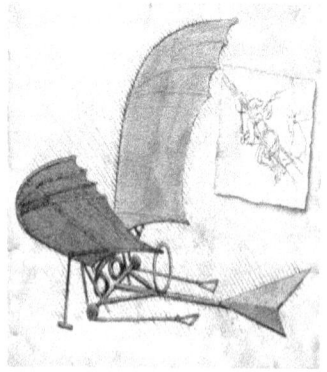

Identify the Pictures

31. On June 28, 2007, it was made a UNESCO World Heritage Site. It is one of the 20th century's most distinctive buildings and one of the most famous performing art centres in the world. Identify the building.

32. The red disc in this country's flag represents the blood of those who died for the independence, and the green field stands for the lushness of the land of this country. Identify.

33. These are the first ever winners of the World Championship in which sport?

34. Identify this sport.

35. On the occasion of Nobel Peace Prize award in 1970, the laureate, Dr. Norman Borlaug, said of this man: "*The green revolution has been a team effort and much of the credit for its spectacular development must go to the Indian officials, Organizations, Scientists and Farmers. However, to you, a great deal of the credit must go for first recognising the potential value of the Mexican dwarfs. Had this not occurred, it is quite possible that there would not have been a green revolution in Asia.*" Identify the man.

36. Name the title of this book.

Identify the Pictures

37. ***Christ the Redeemer*** is considered the largest Art Deco statue in the world. The statue is one of the **New Seven Wonders of the World.** Where is the statue located?

38. The Mazar-e-Quaid (National Mausoleum) is an iconic building in Karachi. While it is the repository for the remains of a number of important personages, it is principally the tomb of which individual?

39. He is best known for his pioneering work in the development of modern Atomic Theory, and his research on Colour Blindness. Identify him.

40. Which company owns the following brands?

41. The manager of the team, Argentina in South Africa World Cup, 2010 shown in the picture is often associated with a phrase, 'Hand of God'? Who is he?

42. Identify the freedom fighter.

Identify the Pictures

43. Name the monument.

44. Which political party's symbol has been illustrated here?

45. Where in Delhi would you find the following museum?

46. Which country's currency has been given here?

47. By what name is this *shloka* called popularly in Sanskrit?

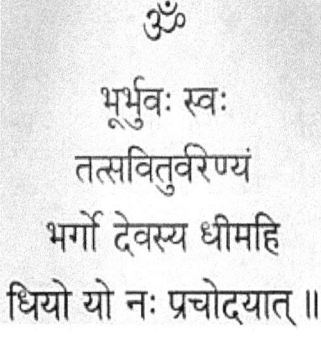

48. He is a legendary British hunter and tracker-turned-conservationist, author and naturalist, famous for hunting a large number of man-eating tigers and leopards in India. Identify him.

Identify the Pictures

49. The stories depicted in the caves shown below are from which epic?

50. The only temple in the world dedicated to the God illustrated below is located in which Indian city?

51. The image shown below depicts Arjuna with 'Gandiva', an incredibly powerful bow. Who presented it to Arjuna?

52. Identify the award.

53. Identify this train that has been specially designed for promoting tourism in Rajasthan.

54. Which famous monument was built by Muhammad Quli Qutub Shah in 1951 to commemorate the end of Plague?

Identify the Pictures

55. In which Indian city would you find the following terminus?

56. A Greek mathematician, physicist, engineer, inventor and astronomer. How do we know him?

57. Identify the emperor who has built the following famous monument.

58. Which country gifted the following statue to the United States of America?

59. After Dr. Sarvepalli Radhakrishnan, he is the only person to be elected as the Vice President of India for two consecutive terms. Who is he?

60. He is the founder of which famous company? Name it.

Identify the Pictures 37

61. She gave a special recital of devotional songs for the Silver Jubilee celebrations of the United Nations in 1970. Identify her.

62. Whose *samadhi* is shown below?

63. She is known for achieving which feat?

64. She founded the *Theosophical Society* and the *Home Rule League*. Who is she?

65. He was a senior leader of the Indian *National Congress (INC)* and founder of the *Servants of India Society*. Identify him.

66. Identify the television series and name it.

Identify the Pictures

67. Name the actress in the picture, who was the first recipient of the *Dada Saheb Phalke* award.

68. Who was the first occupant of this building?

69. The following temple is a place of worship for people of which religion?

70. Identify the painter.

71. She was a Polish physicist and chemist, working mainly in France. She was the first woman to win a Nobel Prize, the only woman to win in two fields, and the only person to win in multiple sciences. How do we popularly know her?

72. She was the first Indian woman to become the *President of the Indian National Congress (INC)* and the first woman to become the *Governor of Uttar Pradesh*. Her birthday is celebrated as the Women's Day all over India. Identify her.

Identify the Pictures

73. He founded the *Swatantra Party* and was one of the first recipients of India's highest civilian award, the *Bharat Ratna*. Identify him.

74. Name the sportsperson.

75. Nur-ud-din Mohammad Salim was the fourth Mughal Emperor who ruled from 1605 until his death in 1627. What was his popular name?

76. Identify the 'Iron Lady'.

77. Following is the flag of which organisation?

78. Name the game.

Identify the Pictures 43

79. The Peruvudaiyar Kovil at Thanjavur in the Indian state of Tamil Nadu, is a Hindu temple dedicated to Lord Shiva. It is an art of the work achieved by which dynasty in Tamil architecture?

80. Identify the two people illustrated below.

81. Name the author of this book.

82. For what reason do we remember this Russian woman?

83. Identify the painter of this painting.

84. Name the author of the given book.

Identify the Pictures

85. Who won the National Award for choreography for this film?

86. In which city did this incident occur?

87. Identify the musical instrument.

88. Which is this famous chocolate?

89. Which fashion brand does the given logo indicate?

90. Recognise the picture illustrated here.

Identify the Pictures

91. The given dance form can be associated with which place?

92. Identify the leaf on the given flag.

93. What do we call this position?

94. Whose best friend is the cartoon figure in the picture?

95. With which country would you associate the given hat?

96. Where would you find this museum?

Identify the Pictures

49

97. The given picture has the founders of which famous company?

98. Name the movie illustrated here.

99. Identify the powerpuff girl, drawn here.

100. Which major river's course is marked on the map?

101. Identify the composer on this Austrian currency.

102. Identify the constellation.

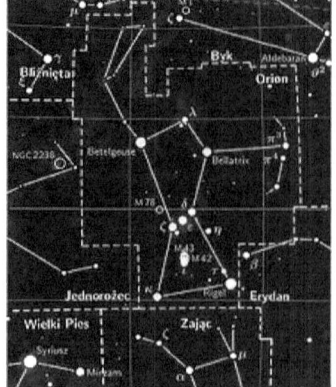

Identify the Pictures

103. This is the logo of which famous browser by Google?

104. This café is inspired by whom?

105. He is best known for his contributions to the evolutionary theory. Who is he?

106. He is best known for the *Bhoodan Movement*. He is considered as a National Teacher of India and the spiritual successor of Mohandas Karamchand Gandhi. Identify him.

107. A fictional protagonist and narrator of a novel written by Jonathan Swift. Who is he?

108. The given picture is the new identity of which sportswear company?

Identify the Pictures

109. The given book is co-authored by _____ and Frederick Engels. Name him.

110. Name the author of the following book.

111. Identify the founder of the *Swatantra Party* shown in the picture.

112. He has been called the 'Frontier Gandhi' by the Indians. Who is he?

113. Identify the Indian vocalist shown in the picture.

114. Name the picture of the building illustrated here.

Identify the Pictures

115. His journey is described in his important travelogue, *A Record of Buddhist Kingdoms*, being an account by the Chinese monk of his Travels in India and Ceylon (Sri Lanka) in search of the Buddhist books of discipline. Identify him.

116. Name the character in the picture given illustrated here.

117. The airport of Patna is named after him. Identify this person.

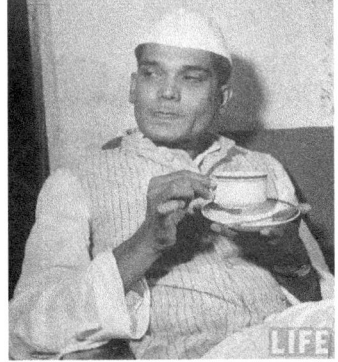

118. Whose driving licence is this?

119. Identify the author of this book, who is also the founder of India's leading IT company.

120. Name this economist who has been appointed as the recent RBI governor.

Identify the Pictures

121. The given picture is the cover of which famous book written in literature by a Nobel Laureate?

122. The given picture is a short astronomical treatise published in New Latin in March 1610. It was the first published scientific work based on observations made through a telescope. Identify the author.

123. Name this river involved in an epic struggle.

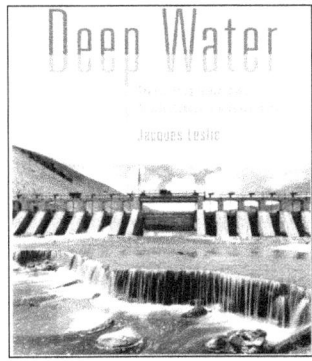

124. Identify and name the movement in the given picture.

125. Name the person in the picture illustrated here.

Identify the Pictures

Answers

1. Wright Brothers
2. Petrie Dish
3. Steel
4. Mangal Pandey
5. Vamana
6. Veena
7. Vijaya Lakshmi Pandit
8. Madhubani
9. Dadasaheb Phalke
10. Chandragupta Maurya
11. Madhya Pradesh
12. Krishnadevaraya
13. Kerala
14. Pashupati Nath
15. Sucheta Kriplani
16. Parimarjan Negi
17. Satyam Shivam Sundaram
18. Dubai
19. XBOX
20. Milkha Singh
21. Orchids
22. Singapore
23. C.V. Raman
24. Leaning Tower of Pisa
25. Paragliding
26. John F. Kennedy
27. Amitabh Bachchan
28. Puri
29. JRD Tata
30. Leonardo da Vinci
31. Sydney Opera House
32. Bangladesh
33. Rubik's Cube Solving
34. Muggle Quidditch
35. Mankombu Sambasivan Swaminathan
36. Megasthenes
37. Rio de Janeiro; Brazil
38. Muhammad Ali Jinnah
39. John Dalton
40. Tata Motors
41. Diego Maradona
42. Lala Lajpat Rai
43. Buland Darwaza
44. NCP
45. Patel Chowk Metro Station
46. UAE
47. Gayatri Mantra
48. Jim Corbett
49. Jataka
50. Pushkar
51. Varuna dev
52. Param Vir Chakra
53. Palace on Wheels

54. Charminar
55. Mumbai
56. Archimedes
57. Shah Jahan
58. France
59. Mohammad Hamid Ansari
60. Infosys
61. M S Subbulaxmi.
62. Charan Singh
63. First woman to cross English channel
64. Annie Besant
65. Gopal Krishna Gokhale
66. Hum Log
67. Devika Rani
68. John Adams
69. Bahai
70. Leonardo da Vinci
71. Madam Curie
72. Sarojini Naidu
73. C. Rajagopalachari
74. Andre Agassi
75. Jahangir
76. Margaret Thatcher
77. UNICEF
78. Angry Birds
79. Cholas
80. Judas and Jesus
81. Leo Tolstoy
82. First woman in space
83. Vincent Van Gogh
84. Rudyard Kipling
85. Shiamak Davar
86. Paris
87. Saxophone
88. Toblerone
89. Gucci
90. Big Ben
91. Hawaii
92. Maple
93. Pirouette
94. Asterix
95. Mexico
96. Paris
97. Google
98. The Godfather
99. Blossom
100. Danube
101. Mozart
102. Orion
103. Chrome
104. Barbie
105. Charles Darwin
106. Vinoba Bhave
107. Gulliver
108. Reebok
109. Karl Marx
110. Abul Fazl
111. C. Rajagopalachari
112. Khan Abdul Ghaffar Khan

Identify the Pictures

113. Bhimsen Gururaj Joshi
114. Sabarmati Ashram
115. Fa-Hien
116. Alice
117. Jayaprakash Narayan
118. J.R.D. Tata
119. Narayan Murthy
120. Raghuraman Rajan
121. Jungle Book
122. Galileo
123. Narmada
124. Chipko Movement
125. Walt Disney

Complete the Sentences with Appropriate Words

1. After the League of Nations failed to prevent the World War II, there was a widespread recognition that humankind could not afford a Third World War. Therefore, _____ was established to replace the flawed League of Nations in 1945 in order to maintain international peace and promote cooperation in solving international economic, social and humanitarian problems.

2. _____ is the only U.S. state to be named after a President.

3. After independence, _____ became the capital of Punjab. Its name has been derived from the Goddess Shyamala Devi, an incarnation of the Hindu Goddess, Kali.

   The Mount Rushmore National Memorial is a sculpture carved into the granite face of Mount Rushmore in the United States. Sculpted by Danish-American Gutzon Borglum and his son, it features sculptures of the heads of four United

   and Abraham Lincoln.

4. Th e*Avesta* is the primary collection of sacred texts of _____ religion.

5. Walt _____ received a special award from the League of Nations for creating Mickey in 1935.

6. _____ was an Indian independence activist and political leader, remembered, especially for leading the opposition against Indira Gandhi in the 1970s and for giving a call for peaceful Total Revolution.

Complete the Sentences...   63

7. The _____ was a fortress in Paris that played an important role in the internal conflicts of France and for most of its history was used as a state prison by the kings of France.

8. Mithun Chakraborty runs _____ newspaper in the film, 'Guru'.

9. ____(a)____ was a city in Ancient India, the capital of the Videha Kingdom. The city of _____(a)__ has been identified as modern day Janakpur in the Dhanusa district of Nepal. The most famous Janaka of (a)_____ was Kushadhwaja, father of _____(b)_____.

10. Machu Picchu voted as one of the New Seven Wonders of the World in a worldwide Internet Poll in 2007 is located in _____.

11. Indira _____ Gandhi was the third Prime Minister of India and a central figure of the Indian National Congress party.

12. In the 1860s, _____ demonstrated the *germ theory of disease* by eliminating bacteria from silkworms. The institute he founded in 1887 is noted for its research into micro-organisms and vaccines.

13. The Aswan Dam is an embankment dam situated across the _____ river in Aswan, Egypt.

14. _____ and Blefuscu are two fictional island nations that appear in the first part of the 1726 novel, *Gulliver's Travels* by Jonathan Swift.

   Jimmy Carter was awarded the 2002 Nobel Peace Prize, the only U.S.

15. During the Roman Republic, the _____ was a list that kept track of all adult males fit for military service.

16. _____ did not realise the significance of many of his inventions when he invented them; today, many are widely used products. He thought little of the safety pin, selling the patent

for a paltry sum of $400 to W R Grace and Company, to pay a man to whom he owed $15.

17. _____ has sold more than 300 million records worldwide and is recognised as the best-selling female recording artist of all time by the Guinness World Records.

18. A former dacoit named 'Ratnakara' composed a famous epic. He is popularly known as _____.

19. The French acquired _____ in 1674 and held control, with occasional interruption from the British and the Dutch, until 1954, when it was incorporated into the Indian Union along with the rest of the French India.

There exists a tomb of Anarkali in Lahore. The gravestone in the tomb for Anarkali bears the tragic inscription:
Could I behold the face of my beloved once more,
I would thank God until the day of resurrection.'

20. _____ was founded in 1636 by vote of the Great and General Court of the Massachusetts Bay Colony, making it the oldest institution of higher learning in the United States.

21. The British captured Delhi in 1857 and the city replaced _____ as the seat of the British government in India in 1911.

22. _____, nicknamed 'The Maid of Orléans', is a folk heroine of France and a Roman Catholic saint.

23. The UAE is an Arab country that is a federation of seven emirates. The constituent emirates are _____, Ajman, _____, Fujairah, Rasal-Khaimah, _____, and Umm al-Quwain.

24. *The Adventures of Tom Sawyer* by Mark Twain is an 1876 novel about a young boy growing up along the _____ river.

25. _____ is an American author of a thriller fiction, best known for the 2003 bestselling novel, *The Da Vinci Code*.

Complete the Sentences...

26. _____ was a South African cardiac surgeon who performed the world's first successful human-to-human heart transplant.

27. _____ was an English poet and playwright, widely regarded as the greatest writer in the English language and the world's pre-eminent dramatist. He is often called England's national poet and the 'Bard of Avon'.

28. In the fictional world of J. K. Rowling's book series, *Harry Potter*, a _____ is a person who lacks any sort of magical ability and was not born into the magical world.

29. _____ was an Indian emperor who ruled northern India from 606 to 647 from his capital, Kannauj.

30. According to one version, the word _____ is derived from a Russian verb, 'rubit', i.e., to cut, to chop, or to hack.

31. _____ in Latin means pebble/abacus. There is a character in Tintin by this name. It is also a modern name in Mathematics.

32. The tournament was conceived in 1899 by four members of the Harvard University tennis team who wished to challenge the British to a tennis competition. Once their respective lawn tennis associations agreed, one of the four Harvard players, Dwight F. _____, designed a tournament format and ordered an appropriate sterling silver trophy from Shreve, Crump & Low, purchasing it from his own funds for about $1000.

33. _____ held the FIDE World Chess Championship from 2000 to 2002, at a time when the world title was split.

34. The _____ is the headquarters of the United States Department of Defence, located in Virginia.

The English name of Singapore is derived from the Malay word, 'Singapura' literally meaning the Lion City. Hence the customary reference to the nation as the Lion City.

35. _____, in a doctor's prescription, is often expressed as 120/80.

36. _____ was the capital city of the Pallava Kingdom between the 4th and 9th centuries. The city is well known for its handwoven silk sarees and most of the city's workforce is involved in the weaving industry.

37. *A Tale of Two Cities* is a novel by Charles Dickens, set in _____ and _____ before and during the French Revolution.

38. _____ was born as Anna Maria Grosholtz in 1761 in France. Her mother worked as a housekeeper for Dr. Philippe Curtius in Switzerland, who was a physician skilled in *wax modelling*. Curtius taught her the art of wax modelling.

39. The Nagarjuna Sagar Dam is a masonry dam on the _____ river in the border of Guntur and Nalgonda districts of Andhra Pradesh.

40. _____ is the most popular city in United States known as the *Sin City* as it caters to various vices.

41. Scandinavia is a historical region in Northern Europe that includes the three kingdoms of _____, Norway and _____.

The 42nd President of the United States, Bill Clinton was born William

42. *Th rille*is the sixth studio album by American recording artist _____. It was released on November 30, 1982, by *Epic Records* as the follow-up to _____, critically and commercially successful 1979 album, *Off the Wall*.

43. The fourth guru of Sikhism, Guru Ram Das, excavated a tank in 1577 CE which subsequently became known as _____ meaning 'Pool of the Nectar of Immortality', giving its name to the city that grew around it.

44. The second line of a very famous song is 'Oh, what fun it is to

Complete the Sentences...

ride in a one horse open sleigh'. The first line is _____.

45. The _____ family is the largest family of flowering plants. The number of _____ species equals to about four times the number of mammal species, or more than twice the number of bird species.

46. After the invention of telephones in 1876, Thomas Alva Edison suggested the word, _____ to start a conversation.

47. _____ is a fictional character created by the Italian writer *Carlo Collodi*. Carved by a woodcarver named, *Geppetto* in a small Italian village, he was created as a wooden puppet, but dreamt of becoming a real boy.

48. _____ is regarded as the 'father of Qawwali'.

49. The _____ were an *English rock band* formed in *Liverpool* in 1960. Their best-known lineup, consisting of John Lennon, Paul McCartney, George Harrison and Ringo Starr were considered by many as the greatest and most influential act of the rock era.

50. _____ is a mythological white elephant who carries the Hindu God, Indra.

51. _____ is a mountain pass in the Aravalli Range of Rajasthan in western India. The name is believed to have come from the yellow coloured soil of this region.

52. In the mid-19th and early 20th century, _____ was the capital of the Punjab region under the British Raj.

53. The _____ is a range of hills in central India. It is a Sanskrit word, which means 'seven mountains'.

54. As the birthplace of Muhammad and a site of Muhammad's first revelation of the Quran, _____ is regarded as the holiest city in the religion of Islam and a pilgrimage to it known as the *Hajj* is obligatory for all the able Muslims.

55. _____ is the headquarters of The Tibetan government-in-exile.

56. _____ composed the music, and sang for two dance sequences in the Satyajit Ray's *Shatranj ke Khiladi*, and choreographed the song, *Kaahe Chhed Mohe* from the 2002 film, *Devdas*.

57. Complete the original title of a book: *'Travels into Several Remote Nations of the World* in Four Parts by Lemuel _____, first a Surgeon, and then a Captain of several Ships.'

58. _____, _____ and _____ were the first recipients of *Bharat Ratna*.

59. Fa-Hien visited India during the reign of _____ and is most known for his pilgrimage to _____, the birthplace of Gautama Buddha in modern Nepal.

60. _____ is an *Apsara* in Hindu legend whose name means 'one who controls the heart'.

Origin of the name 'Baroda'.

It is rumoured that the name, 'Baroda' originated from two words, Vat which means the Banyan tree and Aodh, which means a Tent/canopy. According to a popular legend, the region in and around present day Baroda was full of 'Banyan trees' that formed a dense cover which looked like a huge tent canopy from a distance. Thus the name Baroda came into existence.

61. BISP is a cash transfer programme in Pakistan known as _____ Income Support Programme that is similar to the Direct Benefit Transfer Scheme being launched here in India.

62. The _____ is a teacher of high regard in the 'Gelug or Yellow Hat' school of Tibetan Buddhism, founded by *Tsongkhapa*.

63. Jan Koum and Brian Acton are associated with _____ *mobile chat service.*

64. _____ was launched as 'The Cricket Champion-

Complete the Sentences...

ship of India' following a meeting of the Board of Control for Cricket in India in July 1934 with a donation from Maharaja Bhupinder Singh of Patiala.

65. _____ school was voted as the 36th best Scottish educational establishment in a 2008 online ranking, outranking Edinburgh's Loretto School.

66. _____ is a garden in present Sri. Lanka, the kingdom of demon king Ravana, as mentioned in the Hindu epic, 'Ramayana' of Valmiki. It has garden houses around it, built by Vishwakarma himself.

67. Ronald Ross was awarded the *Nobel Prize in Medicine* for his remarkable work on the disease, _____ in 1902.

68. _____ along with Batukeshwar Dutt threw bombs at the empty treasury benches in the Central Assembly in Delhi on April 8, 1929.

69. _____ is known as the *Father of Indian Constitution*.

70. _____ is the only Prime Minister of India who never faced the Parliament and has a university in Meerut city in Uttar Pradesh named after him.

71. _____ is a style of embroidery from Lucknow that is believed to have been introduced by Nur Jahan, the Mughal Emperor, Jahangir's wife.

72. The collective noun for a group of ants is _____.

73. _____ in ancient India was the capital of the kingdom led by the Pandavas in the Mahabharata epic. It was located upon the banks of the river Yamuna and close to the modern national capital of India, Delhi.

74. _____ was built by Mughal Emperor Akbar in 1572 to commemorate his conquest of Gujarat. A Persian inscription on the eastern archway of the gateway records, Akbar's

conquest of the Deccan in 1601. It is also known as the 'Gate of Magnificence'.

75. _____ is commonly used to refer to the Indian sage, Vardhamana.

76. In the the Hindi saying, 'Gharkābhedi Lankadhāe', _____ is the 'Gharkābhedi', who destroyed Lanka.

77. _____ is depicted on all Pakistani rupee notes of denominations five and higher, and is the namesake of many Pakistani public institutions.

78. _____ was constructed in 1527 by the order of Babur on Ramkot Hill ('Rama's fort') and was destroyed in 1992.

79. _____ was the author of the revered great *Mantra* - The *Gayatri Mantra* and is the preceptor of Rama in the Indian epic, *Ramayana*.

80. Maharaja Sawai Pratap Singh built _____ in 1799 that has a unique five-store exterior that is akin to the honeycomb of the beehive with its 953 small windows called *jharokhas* that are decorated with intricate lattice work.

written by J. K. Rowling. The organisation is headquartered at 12 Grimmauld Place, London.

81. _____ was born to *Anjana* and *Kesari* on *Mula Nakshatra*, on the full moon day in the month of *Chaitra* near *Trimbakeshwar, Maharashtra*.

82. _____ was established outside Dehradun by the *Prince of Wales* as a *feeder school for Indians* headed to the Royal Military Academy at Sandhurst, England in 1922.

83. According to a Hindu legend, once Lord Shiva opened his eyes after a long time of *dhyana*, because of extreme fulfilment, he

Complete the Sentences...

shed out a drop of tear and this single tear from Shiva's eye grew into a tree named _____ .

84. _____ was appointed by Iltutmish as his successor making her the first woman to rule India.

85. _____ in Gujarat has the following: *Hridaya Kunj, Nandini, Vinoba Kutir* and *Upasana Mandir.*

86. According to the Jain tradition, _____ was the 24th and the last Tirthankara.

87. The Union Finance Minister presents the budget in the _____.

88. The word, _____ comes from the Greek word, meaning 'rule of the people' and our India is the best example of it.

89. _____ was nominated by the Government of India for the post of *UN Secretary General* in 2006. His doctoral thesis, 'Reasons of State', is still prescribed reading in courses on Indian foreign-policy making.

90. The International Airport in Delhi is named after_____.

91. Vaiko, a prominent Tamil politician, was controversially arrested under the POTA for his support to the *Liberation Tigers of Tamil Eelam (LTTE)*. *POTA* stands for _____.

92. On January 30, 1948, Gandhiji was shot and killed by _____, while having his nightly public walk on the grounds of the Birla House in New Delhi. The assassin was a Hindu radical with links to the extremist Hindu Mahasabha who held Gandhi responsible for weakening India by insisting upon a payment to Pakistan.

93. _____ leads the National Congress Party (NCP) who was earlier a member of the Congress.

94. The American President _____ is associated with the slogan 'Yes We Can'.

95. _____ was the last Governor-General of India and the only Indian to hold that office.

96. _____ is the upper house of the Bicameral United States Congress that derives its name from a Latin word meaning, 'Council of Elders'.

97. Located at 1600 Pennsylvania Avenue NW in Washington D.C., the house was designed by Irish-born James Hoban, and built between 1792 and 1800 of white-painted Aquia sandstone in the Neoclassical style is the residence of _____.

98. Before the independence of India and Pakistan, _____ was closely associated with the founders of the Aligarh Movement. After the independence of Pakistan, the founder of Pakistan, Mohammad Ali Jinnah frequently wore it and made it the national dress of Pakistan.

99. _____ means the body of people (in an institutional sense), who would meet to discuss the matters of state.

100. _____ is derived from the Latin word, *coquere* meaning 'to cook' and refers to a specific set of cooking traditions and practices, often associated with a specific culture.

101. In Egypt, Lebanon and Syria, it is known as *'Zalabia'*. Th is sweet is called 'jeri' in Nepal, a word derived from *Jangiri*, and the Mughul Emperor, Jahangir. In Morocco, Algeria and Tunisia this sweet is known as *Zlebia* or *Zlabia*. It is called _____ in India.

102. We know it as *Panipuri* in Western India, *Gol Gappa* in Northern India and _____ in Bengali.

the sun).

Complete the Sentences...

103. _____ is a salad dressing that gets its name from the Mediterranean city of Mahon, where it was first made.

104. _____ was concocted by a pharmacist named Caleb D. Bradham as a cure for *dyspepsia*.

105. _____ is the method of cooking food that uses a small amount of fat in a shallow pan over relatively high heat.

106. A patent for the _____ was registered on May 31, 1894 under the name, Granose by Dr. John Harvey Kellogg, the superintendent of The Battle Creek Sanitarium in Battle Creek, Michigan.

107. When the British first introduced _____ in India, the Indians called them *double roti*. This term has today become the broad term for all types of leavened bread.

108. _____ is the pejorative term for source code which has a complex and tangled control structure, especially one using many GOTOs, exceptions, threads, or other 'unstructured' branching constructs. It is named after a popular Italian food item that is twisted and tangled.

109. The word, _____ owes its origin to a French verb meaning 'to restore'.

110. The name of the brand _____ is derived from the name of an Indian Railway station in Mumbai, where the production factory of the brand is based.

111. In French, the term _____ came to be applied to a detailed list or 'résumé' of any kind. It is related to the food industry.

112. The established French classifications of _____ are bouillon and consommé.

113. Ingredients: Kashmiri green tea 4 tsps, saffron 2-4 strands, crushed green cardamom pods 2, blanched and chopped al-

monds 8, cinnamon 1 stick, cloves 1-2, sugar 2 tbsps or to taste, The above is the recipe for the beverage _____ .

114. *The eInternational Dyslexia Association*, screened the movie _____ (produced by Aamir Khan Productions) on October 29, 2008 in the United States.

115. _____ played the role of Natasha, a.k.a. Linda in the movie, 'Kites'.

116. Managing director of *Maratha Mandir* said, "The film completes 14 years in our cinema hall and we still get at least 60-70% occupancy on weekdays and a houseful board on weekend and holidays. _____ is the film that has been screened at *Maratha Mandir* for 14 years.

The origin of Pav Bhaji can be traced to textile mill workers in Mumbai in the 1850s.

The mill workers used to have lunch breaks too short for a full meal, and a light lunch was preferred to a heavy one, as the employees had to return to strenuous physical labour after lunch. A vendor created this dish using items or parts of other dishes available on the menu. Roti or rice was replaced with pav and the curries that usually go with the Indian bread or rice, and all these were amalgamated into just one spicy concoction, the bhaji. Initially, it remained the food of the mill-workers. With time, the dish found its way into restaurants and spread over Central Mumbai and other parts of the city via the Udupi restaurants.

117. _____ was an actor whose birth name was Abhas Kumar Ganguly. He was the second youngest of the four siblings, the other three being Ashok (the eldest), Sati Devi and Anoop.

118. In the movie _____, you come across a computer programmer, 'Neo' who is drawn into a rebellion against the machines.

119. _____ is a film directed by Steven Spielberg that centres on the fictional, Isla Nublar in Costa Rica, where billionaire philanthropist, John Hammond and a team of

Complete the Sentences...

genetic scientists from his company have created an amusement park.

120. The profession of Vidya Balan was _____ in the movie, '*Lage Raho Munnabhai*'.

121. _____ is made of gold-plated britannium on a black metal base, and is 13.5 inches (34 cm) tall, weighs 8.5 lb (3.85 kg) and depicts a knight rendered in Art Deco style holding a crusader's word standing on a reel of film with five spokes. The five spokes, each represent the original branches of the American Academy of Motion Picture Arts and Sciences: Actors, Writers, Directors, Producers and Technicians.

122. _____ is referred to as the 'Mozart of Madras' by the *Time magazine* and several Tamil commentators have coined him the nickname, *Isai Puyal* meaning, *Music Storm*.

123. Pop artist _____ co-wrote the charity single, "We Are the World" in 1985 with Lionel Richie, which was released worldwide to aid the poor in the United States and Africa.

124. Satyajit Ray's first film was_____ that won eleven international prizes, including the Best Human Document at the Cannes Film Festival.

125. _____ was the writer and director of the Flop Show, an Indian television sitcom that first aired on Doordarshan in 1989.

126. _____ won the *Miss India title in 1984* and is the co-owner of the *Indian Premier League* team, *Kolkata Knight Riders* in partnership with Shahrukh Khan under their company, Red Chillies Entertainment.

127. _____ has choreographed the dance numbers: *Cholike-Peeche from Khlanayak* and *Ek Do Teen* from *Tezaab*.

128. _____ is a Delhi-based band, whose name means, 'orbital revolutions' in Sanskrit. Their first song, 'Xerox' was named 'the face of Indian rock'. Nitin Malik is their lead vocalist.

129. _____ is a supersonic cruise missile whose name is perceived as the confluence of the two nations represented by two rivers, the *Brahmaputra of India* and the *Moskva of Russia*.

130. _____ fabric derives its name from the Latin for the flax plant.

131. _____ was produced under the guidance of Dr. P. K. Sethi by Masterji Ram Chander in 1969 for victims of landmine explosions and is used for people with below-knee amputations.

132. _____ is referred to as the Western Father of Medicine in recognition of his lasting contributions to the field and is widely known for being the writer of the oath historically taken by doctors swearing to practice medicine ethically.

133. _____ gas is added by the soft drink companies to their beverages during the manufacturing process so as to cause the drink to 'fizz'.

134. _____ in Latin means of or from cows and was first used by *Edward Jenner* (an English physician) in 1796.

135. _____ was a *Russian chemist and inventor* who was credited as being the creator of the first version of *the periodic table of elements*.

136. Complete the following book title: .... - *A Biography of the World's Most Famous Equation*.

137. The word, _____ was coined by Oliver Wendell Holmes, Sr. in 1846 and means 'Without Sensation'.

138. _____ was invented by LászlóBíró, a Hungarian newspaper editor, who was frustrated by the amount of time that he wasted in filling up fountain pens.

Complete the Sentences...

139. _____ was formerly called marsh fever due to its association with swamps and marshland and its name originates from Medieval Italian - 'bad air'.

140. _____ treatise, on floating bodies, 'Proposition 5', states that 'Any floating object displaces its own weight of fluid.

141. _____ is the author of the book, *Philosophiæ Naturalis Principia Mathematica*, Latin for "Mathematical Principles of Natural Philosophy written in 1687 that laid the groundwork for most of the classical mechanics.

142. The chemical name for vitamin _____ is derived from the Latin name of scurvy, 'scorbutus'.

and Uncle Topolino are tributes to Mickey, as Topolino (meaning "little

143. The former American professional basketball player _____ has earned the nickname, 'His Airness' because of his leaping ability.

144. With this sport, you associate the terms: butterfly, breaststroke, freestyle and backstroke. It is _____.

145. A singles player or doubles team achieve a _____ if they win the Australian Open, the French Open, the Wimbledon and the US Open in the same year.

146. _____ plays as a winger or a forward for Spanish Club, Real Madrid and serves as captain of the Portuguese national team.

147. The _____ award is presented by the government of India for excellence in sports coaching.

148. The Indian city, _____ meaning 'Meadow of Flowers' became the host for the *2010 Commonwealth Winter Games*.

149. _____ is the only German to have won the *Formula One* championship and is currently driving for Mercedes GP.

150. _____ is a team contact sport that originated in India. It is often chanted during the game and derives its name from a Hindi word meaning 'holding of breath'.

151. The fouls in the fictional game, _____ are classified as Blagging, Blatching, Blurting, Bumphing, Cobbing, Flacking, Haversacking, Quaffle-pocking, Snitchnip, Stooging, etc.

152. In the world of tennis, _____ is often referred to as *Fed Express* or the *Swiss Maestro*.

153. "After talking with my children, my family and my closest friends, I have decided to return to professional cycling in order to raise awareness of the global cancer burden", said _____. His words can be found on his *livestrong band.*

154. The martial art form, _____ was developed in the Ryukyu Islands in Japan.

155. _____ is regarded as one of the greatest athletes India has ever produced and is often called the 'Queen of Indian track and field'. She is nicknamed as *Payyoli Express*.

156. *Fed Cup* is the premier team competition in women's tennis. _____ is the men's equivalent of Fed Cup.

157. The slang used for a fastball that is especially hard to hit due to its velocity and/or movement in baseball is _____. It is named after an analgesic used to relieve minor aches and pains.

158. The *Guinness World Records* has consistently listed the fictional detective _____ as the 'most portrayed movie character' with over 70 actors playing the part in over 200 films. It was inspired by Dr. Joseph Bell and is famous for his intellectual prowess, and is renowned for his skilful use of 'deductive reasoning'.

159. _____ is a gift, mandatory in Islam, given by the groom to the bride upon marriage in Islamic cultures.

160. Lord Rama with his wife, Sita and brother Laxman was said to have cut off the nose of Ravana's sister, Shurpanakha here, thus

giving the city its name as _____.

161. The inspiration for the comic strip, _____ came from Dennis Ketcham, the real life son of Hank Ketcham, who was only four years old when he refused to take a nap and somehow messed up his whole room.

Sarala Devi Chowdhurani — Tagore's niece — intoned the song, along with a few school students, in front of the gathering of the then INC President, Bishan Narayan Dhar.

before the public under the title, Bharata-vidhata in Tottvobodhini Patrika

that month, in a Mahotsava ceremony, it was sung again at the bard's Jorasanko residence.

162. The word, _____ owes its origin to Bengali language and is used elliptically for a 'house in the Bengal style'.

163. The term, _____ is used in a popular boardgame that is an alteration of the Persian phrase, 'ShāhMāt' which means literally, 'the King is ambushed'.

164. _____ is a minor goddess, and the wife of *Agni*. Her three sons Pavak, Pavamana and Shuchi consume the oblations offered to the fire during sacrifices.

165. Stuart Robertson who was working as the marketing manager of England and Wales Cricket Board proposed the idea of _____ in 2002 and it was put to vote which was passed by 11 votes to 7.

166. _____ is a site of an ancient forest, which is the region where Lord Krishna spent his childhood days. It is nicknamed as the 'City of Widows' after the large population of abandoned widows who seek refuge here. .

167. 'Operation West End' was a sting operation aimed at sensationalising the corruption underlying India's large defence con-

tracts and forced India's defense minister - George Fernandes to resign. The publication that was behind this sting operation was _____.

168. _____ came to be known as '*Kashyap Marga*' when Rishi Kashyap drained out the water of the lake making the submerged land a *habitable valley*.

169. In 1816, the French physician, Rene Theoplhie Laennec introduced a perforated wooden cylinder, which concentrated the sounds of air flowing in and out of the lungs, and described the sound which it revealed. This invention laid the foundation for development of the modern form of the instrument, known as _____.

170. _____ is a politician whose best-known Hindi film is *Izzat* and has also acted in the English movie, 'Epistle' released in 1961, produced by *Shankar Giri*, son of former president of India Dr. V.V. Giri.J.

171. The Birla Institute of Technology & Science, Pilani was founded by the late Dr. Ghanshyam Das Birla in 1929 as an intermediate college in the state of _____.

172. _____ was first introduced as 'Brad's Drink' in New Bern, North Carolina in 1898 by Caleb Bradham, who made it at his pharmacy, where the drink was sold. Tropicana, Cheetos, Frito – lays and Aquafina are few of the famous brands of this company.

173. _____ is surname of Indian origin that means 'headman' or 'village chief'. It is derived from a word meaning the record keeper named by princely rulers in Gujarat to keep track of the crops.

174. Her action of refusing to give her seat sparked the Montgomery Bus Boycott. U.S. Congress called her 'the first lady of civil rights', and 'the mother of the freedom movement'. She is _____ .

Complete the Sentences...

175. In Leicester (England), there is a park with the slogan, 'South Africa belongs to all those who live there, Black and White'. This park is named after _____.

176. The Pashupatinath temple is the one of the biggest Hindu temple in the world located on the banks of the Bagmati River in the eastern part of Kathmandu. This temple is dedicated to _____.

177. In the Seinfeld episode, 'The Good Samaritan,' Jerry proposes that one should say, 'You're so good looking!' in response to a sneeze in lieu of the phrase _____.

178. The Totapuri mango is the only breed of mango used to make the commercial product _____.

179. The term _____ comes from the old French desport meaning 'leisure'.

founding of the city of Singapore. He is often described as the "Father of

180. Th *Patanwas* was the capital of Gujarat in the medieval times. This city in Gujarat has given name to one of the finest hand-woven sarees called _____ .

181. On the occasion of the receipt of the *Nobel Peace Prize in 1970*, Dr. Norman Borlaug said of this person: "The Green Revolution has been a team effort and much of the credit for its spectacular development must go to the Indian officials, Organizations, Scientists and farmers. However, to you, a great deal of the credit must go for first recognising the potential value of the *Mexican dwarfs*. Had this not occurred, it is quite possible that there would not have been a *Green Revolution in Asia*". This person is _____.

182. The boardgame _____ is named after an economic concept that implies the domination of a market by a single entity.

183. There are two official languages of Sri Lanka. One of them is *Sinhalese* and the other one is _____.

184. The *Varna system of the Hindu society* is described in the text, _____ that reflects the laws and society of the Maurya period in India.

185. _____ is the concept of liberation known in Buddhism that is referred to as 'the highest happiness' and is the goal of the Buddhist path.

186. He is an Indian steel tycoon, philanthropist, and the chairman and chief executive officer of *Arcelor Mittal*. He is the richest man in London and the fifth richest man in the world. He was born in Churu district, Rajasthan, and started his career in 1976 in the family steel business. He is _____.

187. The company _____ is an American computer software company known for its softwares like *Acrobat Reader, Photoshop* and *Flash Player*.

188. The motto of _____ is "Fidelity, Bravery, and Integrity." The headquarters of this organisation, the J. Edgar Hoover Building, is located in Washington, D.C.

189. _____ accorded the title of 'Mahatma' to Mohandas Karamchand Gandhi.

190. Nobel laureate _____ was responsible for producing the first man-made gene in his laboratory in the early seventies.

191. Designed by Sir Edwin Lutyens, it was originally known as the All India War Memorial. This structure situated in Delhi is known as _____.

192. The word _____ is derived from the Japanese words, meaning 'Empty' and 'Orchestra'.

193. _____ is a symbologist in the fiction novel The *Da Vinci Code* written by American author, 'Dan Brown'.

194. _____ was a leader born as *Manikarnika* to a Maharashtrian, Karhade Brahmin and died on 18th June,

Complete the Sentences with Appropriate Words

1858 during the battle of Gwalior.

195. Designed by Christopher Latham Sholes, modern-day keyboard layout for keyboards takes its name from the first six characters seen in the far left of the keyboard's top row of letters. The layout is known as _____ .

Kazakhstan is the world's largest landlocked country by land area and the ninth largest country in the world; its territory of 2,727,300 square kilometres is larger than Western Europe.

196. 'De Dekhudakenaam Per' was the first song of the Indian cinema, and was sung by actor, Wazir Mohammed Khan, from the movie _____.

197. This discipline's name literally translates as 'wind-water' in English. The original designation for the discipline is *Kan Yu* as it uses the laws of both Heaven and Earth to help one improve life by receiving positive energy flow. This Chinese discipline is known as _____.

198. _____ is the most common password used on the internet, while creating user accounts.

199. _____ was the founding editor of the famous newspaper, *Kesari*.

200. The mutiny of _____ broke out from the city of Meerut.

Answers

1. United Nations
2. Washington
3. Shimla
4. Zoroastrianism
5. Disney
6. Jayaprakash Narayan
7. Bastille
8. Swatantra
9. (a) Mithila (b) Sita
10. Peru
11. Priyadarshini
12. Louis Pasteur
13. Nile
14. Lilliput
15. Census
16. Walter Hunt
17. Madonna
18. Valmiki
19. Puducherry
20. Harvard University
21. Kolkata
22. Joan of Arc
23. Abu Dhabi, Dubai, Sharjah
24. Mississippi
25. Dan Brown
26. Barnard
27. William Shakespeare
28. Muggle
29. HarshaVardhana
30. Ruble
31. Calculus
32. Davis
33. Vishwanathan Anand
34. Pentagon
35. Blood Pressure
36. Kanchipuram
37. London and Paris
38. MadamTussaud
39. Krishna
40. Las Vegas
41. Denmark and Sweden
42. Michael Jackson
43. Amritsar
44. Jingle bells, Jingle bells, Jingle all the way
45. Orchid
46. Hello
47. Pinocchio
48. Amir Khusrow
49. Beatles
50. Airavata
51. Haldighati
52. Lahore
53. Satpura
54. Mecca

Complete the Sentences...

55. McLeod Ganj.
56. Pandit Birju Maharaj
57. Gulliver
58. S. Radhakrishnan, C.V. Raman, C. Rajagopalachari
59. Chandragupta II, Lumbini
60. Urvashi
61. Benazir
62. Dalai Lama
63. Whatsapp
64. Ranji Trophy
65. Hogwarts
66. Ashok Vatika
67. Malaria
68. Bhagat Singh
69. Dr. B. R. Ambedkar
70. Charan Singh
71. Chikan
72. Colony
73. Indraprastha
74. Buland Darwaza
75. Mahavira
76. Vibhishan
77. Muhammad Ali Jinnah
78. Babri Masjid
79. Vishvamitra
80. Hawa Mahal
81. Hanuman
82. IMA
83. Rudraksha
84. Razia Sultan
85. Sabarmati Ashram
86. Mahavira
87. Lok Sabha
88. Democracy
89. Shashi Tharoor
90. Indira Gandhi
91. Prevention of Terrorist Activities
92. Nathuram Godse
93. Sharad Pawar
94. Barack Obama
95. C. Rajagopalachari
96. Senate
97. US President
98. Sherwani
99. Parliament
100. Cuisine
101. Jalebi
102. Phuchka
103. Mayonnaise
104. Pepsi
105. Sautéing
106. Corn flakes
107. Sandwich
108. Spaghetti code
109. Restaurant
110. Parle G
111. Menu
112. Clear Soups
113. Kahwah

114. Taare Zameen Par
115. Barbara Mori
116. Dilwale Dulhania Le Jayenge
117. Kishore Kumar
118. Matrix
119. Jurassic Park
120. Radio Jockey
121. Oscar statuette
122. A.R. Rehman
123. Michael Jackson
124. Pather Panchali
125. Jaspal Bhatti
126. Juhi Chawla
127. Saroj Khan
128. Parikrama
129. Brah Mos
130. Linen
131. Jaipur Foot
132. Hippocrates
133. Carbon Dioxide
134. Vaccination
135. Dmitri Mendeleev
136. $E=mc^2$
137. Anaesthesia
138. Ballpoint Pen
139. Malaria
140. Archimedes
141. Isaac Newton
142. Vitamin C
143. Michael Jordan
144. Swimming
145. Grand Slam
146. Cristiano Ronaldo
147. Dronacharya
148. Gulmarg
149. Michael Schumacher
150. Kabaddi
151. Quidditch
152. Roger Federer
153. Lance Armstrong
154. Karate
155. P.T. Usha
156. Davis Cup
157. Aspirin
158. Sherlock Holmes
159. Mahr
160. Nashik
161. Dennis the Menace
162. Bungalow
163. Checkmate
164. Svaha
165. Twenty20 cricket
166. Vrindavan
167. Tehelka
168. Kashmir
169. Stethoscope
170. J. Jayalalitha
171. Rajasthan
172. Pepsi
173. Patel

Complete the Sentences...

174.	Rosa Parks	188.	FBI
175.	Nelson Mandela	189.	Rabindranath Tagore
176.	Lord Shiva	190.	Dr. Hargobind Khorana
177.	God Bless You	191.	India Gate
178.	Frooti	192.	Karaoke
179.	Sport	193.	Robert Langdon
180.	Patola Sarees	194.	Rani Laxmibai of Jhansi
181.	M.S. Swaminathan	195.	Qwerty
182.	Monopoly	196.	Alam Ara
183.	Tamil	197.	Fengshui
184.	Manusmriti	198.	Password
185.	Nirvana	199.	Lokmanya Tilak
186.	Lakshmi Niwas Mittal	200.	1857
187.	Adobe Sytems		

CROSSWORD - 1

CROSSWORD - 1

Across

1. This game is derived from the Indian game, *pachisi*.
2. The oldest tournament of this game is still played on grass. Spencer care was the winner in all tournaments.
3. A 1979 soviet – Indian joint film starring Dharmendra and Hema Malini, was largely based on this adventure tale.
4. A fictional character in the comic series by Belgian cartoonist, Merge.
5. This musical instrument literally nears three strings.

Down

6. A fictional protagonist of Seoul written by Jonathan Swift.
7. A Greek God who bore the weight of the world and the heaven on his shoulder.
8. Spain produces 43.8% of world production of oil produced from this species of tree. It literally means oil from/of Europe.
9. Most populous city in Norway.
10. National language of Sri Lanka.

CROSSWORD - 2

CROSSWORD - 2

Across

1. This city is known as the 'Sin City of Asia' for its level of sex tourism.
2. The name of this instrument translates to 'Beautiful sound' or 'Melody' in Persian.
3. It was named by the Roman senate in horror of the Roman general, Caesar, it being the month of his birth.
4. Second astrological sign in the Zodiac.
5. Second largest U.S State, behind Alaska.

Down

6. This actress was married to Rajnish Behl from 1959 till her death due to cancer in 1991.
7. This place is the birthplace of the religion known as 'Dine-llahi'.
8. One who is the father of this sport can be referred to as a 'toxophilite'.
9. Mansa Devi is the daughter of this Hindu God and is known for her bad temper.
10. *Raghuvamsa* is an epic poem by this celebrated Sanskrit poet.

CROSSWORD - 3

CROSSWORD - 3

Across

1. Gary player is widely regarded as one of the greatest players in the history of this game.
2. This city is a home to the Mayo College that was founded by the British Regime to educate the children of India's royalty.
3. This capital city was originally known as Edo, which means *estuary*.
4. *Argentina's Inventor's Day* is celebrated on Laszle Biro's birthday, September 29. He invented _____.

Down

5. The atomic number of this element is 26.
6. Euclid is the father of this branch of Mathematics.
7. These are organised and overseen by the Academy of Motion Picture Arts and Sciences (AMPAS).
8. This city is known worldwide for its Leaning Tower.
9. This musical instrument rests in the hands of Goddess Saraswati.
10. This river, also called the Rewa, is a river in central India and its name means, 'The giver of pleasure'.

CROSSWORD - 4

CROSSWORD - 4

Across

1. The capital of this country is the only city in the world to contain in its interior a whole state.
2. This Mauryan king was referred to as 'Amitraghata'.
3. This textile made from the fibres of the flax plant was used for wrapping Egyptian mummies.
4. This country's highest peak is Mount Ararat.
5. *Rang de basanti* depicted the use of these fighter aircrafts in defence forces.

Down

6. Napoleon fought his waterloo in this country.
7. Acetylsalicylic acid is better known by this name.
8. Cat Canine, Dog : Feline, Horse:_____
9. The traditional view is that the form of verse, 'shloka' occurred to this poet on seeing a hunter shoot down one of the two birds in love.
10. This bird has the largest known wingspan.

CROSSWORD - 5

CROSSWORD - 5

Across

1. The Bhakra Nangal Dam is a concrete gravity dam across this river.
2. This city is famous in India by the name of the 'City of Weaves'.
3. The world's largest fish market lies in this country.
4. She made her Bollywood debut as a child artist in the film, *Julie* (1975) and as a lead actress in *Solva Sawan* (1978)
5. A fictional town in India created by R.K. Narayan.
6. India's central agency to conduct the Civil Services Examination.

Down

7. His son, Parikshit was born after his death in the Mahabharata war.
8. ECG is a trans thoracic interpretation of the electric activity of this part of the human body over a period of time.
9. One of the three major rivers in the peninsular India that runs from east to west.
10. He is infamously known as the 'Emperor', who 'fiddled, while Rome burnt'.

CROSSWORD - 6

CROSSWORD - 6

Across

1. The Kolanka cup, the tallest sports trophy in the world, is awarded in this sport
2. This e-commerce website was founded as Auction Web in 1995 by Piere Omidyar.
3. Student of Plato and teacher of Alexander the Great.
4. That Central Banking Institution that was set up in 1953 based on the recommendations of the Hilton Young Commission
5. Mother of all the *Devas*.
6. This word is derived from a Latin word, meaning, 'A Breeding' 'a bringing up', 'a rearing'.
7. The Open Source Software released by Linus Torvalds on October 5, 1991.

Down

8. A word related to astronomy that is derived from the Greek word for 'wonderer' because it changes its position in the story
9. The first nation to be created after the second world war
10. The Buddhist Jataka tales were first told in this language

CROSSWORD - 7

CROSSWORD - 7

Across

1. This 2004 Bollywood action thriller film directed by Sanjay Gadhvi with ACP, Jai Dixit as its central character
2. Her full name is Barbara Millicent Roberts and has an on – off love affair with Ken Carson
3. The etymology of this word has a mixed Latin and Greek origin, meaning 'for sight'
4. Italian brand of scooter manufactured by Vespa
5. Motto of this organization is Fidelity, Bravery, Integrity
6. This flightless bird has the following types – little, king, Macaroni, Rock hopper, Emperor

Down

7. The most controversial reform implemented under this Governor General was the policy of taking all legal means possible to assume control over lapsed states
8. China : Triads, Japan : Yakuza, Italy : _____
9. The Indian epic, Mahabharata refers to this state as 'Goparashtra' or 'Govarashtra' which means 'a nation of cowherds'
10. The month of the year named after 'The God of the Doorway'

CROSSWORD - 8

CROSSWORD - 8

Across

1. He made the Raigarh Fort his capital in 1674 when he was crowned the king of the Maratha Kingdom.
2. The Tomb of Itimad-ud-Daulah resides in this Indian city.
3. He constructed the Alamgiri Gate of the Lahore Fort, which is today a UNESCO World Heritage site.
4. A short text describing a deceased person inscribed on his/her tombstone or plaque.
5. A legendary show girl who was born as Nadira Begum or Sharf-un-Nissa.

Down

6. In the 1970s, the comic strip artist, Jim Davis authored *Strip Grom Gnat*, which met with little success, but with some advice from the editor, he created this *new cartoon strip with a cat* as its main character.
7. Her name is one of the Sanskrit words for mountain that refers to her being born the daughter of Himavan.
8. The International Court of Justice of the UN is headquartered in this city.
9. He is the father of the first ruler of Taxila.
10. An element named after the Greek God of the Sun.

CROSSWORD - 9

CROSSWORD - 9

Across

1. Known as the 'city of prime ministers' because from the post independence era, 7 of 13 prime ministers belonged to this city.
2. In thousand and one nights, he recounts his adventures on seven voyages.
3. This word means, 'Water former' in Greek.
4. This social networking website is owned by Google.
5. In 2011, this company entered the alphabet market with the CANVAS series.
6. A German fairytale that was first published in 1812 in the first edition of *Grimm's fairytales*.

Down

7. In a leap year, this festival is celebrated on the 360th day.
8. The social group of this animal is called a 'Pride'.
9. The words that read the same forward or backward.
10. The popular game, Badminton originated in this country.

CROSSWORD - 10

CROSSWORD - 10

Across

1. Lusaka is the capital of this country.
2. A Chinese teacher and philosopher who is most commonly known as Kongzi (literally Master Kong) in Chinese language.
3. A system of alternative medicine created in 1796 by Samuel Hahnemann based on his doctorine of *'Like cures like'*.
4. Japan is known by this name in the Japanese language.
5. Charlie Brown's pet dog created by Charles M. Schulz in the long running comic strip, 'Peanuts'.
6. Half a byte in computer language is better known by this name.

Down

7. It is commonly thought that the name of this country is derived from name of the Qin dynasty.
8. The history of this board game can be traced back to 1903, when an American woman created a game named, 'The Landlord's Game' through which she helped to be able to explain the *single tax theory of Henry George*.
9. Nowshak is the highest point of this country
10. This city was destroyed several times by fire and was renamed 'Christiana' in the honour of King Christian, The 4th.

Answers

CROSSWORD - 1

		¹L	U	D	⁸O			
					L	⁹O		
	²T	E	N	N	I	S		
⁶G					V	L		
U					E	O		
L								¹⁰T
L		³,⁷A	L	I	B	A	B	A
⁴T	I	N	T	I	N			M
V		L						I
E		A						L
R		⁵,³S	I	T	A	R		

CROSSWORD - 2

		¹B	⁸A	N	G	K	O	¹⁰K
	²S	A	R	O	D			A
			C			³J	U	L	Y
⁶N			H					I
U			E					D
⁴T	⁷A	U	R	U	⁹S			A
A	G		Y		H			S
N	R				I			
	A				V			
			⁵T	E	X	A	S	

CROSSWORD - 3

	¹,⁶G	O	L	F			⁹V	
	E			²A	J	M	E	R
³T	O	K	Y	⁷O		⁴,⁸P	E	¹⁰N
	M			S		I	N	A
	E			C		S	A	R
⁵I	T			A		A		M
R	R			R				A
O	Y			S				D
N								A

CROSSWORD - 4

¹I	T	⁷A	L	Y				¹⁰A
		S		⁸E				L
		P		Q		⁹V		B
	²,⁶B	I	N	D	U	S	A	R	A
	E	R		I		L		T
	³L	I	N	E	N	M		R
	G	N		E		I		O
	I					K		S
⁴T	U	R	K	E	Y	I		S
	⁵M	I	G					

CROSSWORD - 5

					¹S	U	⁹T	L	E	J
	²P	⁷A	N	I	P	A	T			
		B		³J	A	P	A	¹⁰N		
		H				T		E		
⁴S	R	I	D	⁸E	V	I		R		
		M		C				O		
	⁵M	A	L	G	U	D	I			
		N								
		Y								
		⁶U	P	S	C					

CROSSWORD - 6

¹,⁸P	O	L	O			¹⁰P	
L				²E	B	A	Y
³A	R	⁹I	S	T	O	T	L	E
N		S				I	
E		⁴R	B	I			
T		⁵A	D	I	T	I	
		⁶E	D	U	C	A	T	I	O	N
		⁷L	I	N	U	X	

CROSSWORD - 7

		¹,⁷D	H	O	O	M			¹⁰J
	²B	A	R	B	I	E		⁹G	A
³T	E	L	E	V	I	S	I	O	N
		H						A	U
		O							A
		U				⁸M			R
⁴V	E	S	P	A		A			Y
⁵F	B	I				F			
	⁶P	E	N	G	U	I	N	S	
						A			

CROSSWORD - 8

		⁷P		¹S	⁸H	I	V	A	J	I
⁶G		²A	G	R	A					
³A	U	R	A	N	G	Z	E	⁹B		
R		V			U			H		
F		A			E			A		
I		T						R		¹⁰H
⁴E	P	I	T	A	P	H		A		E
L								T		L
D			⁵A	N	A	R	K	A	L	I
										U
										M

CROSSWORD - 9

		⁹P						¹⁰I
		A						N
	¹A	L	L	A	H	A	B	A	D
	²S	I	N	D	B	A	D	
⁷C		N						A
³H	Y	D	R	O	G	E	N	
R		R						
I		⁴O	R	K	U	T		
S		⁵M	I	C	R	O	M	A	X
T	⁸L	E						
M	I							
A	O							
⁶S	N	O	W	W	H	I	T	E

CROSSWORD - 10

	¹Z	A	M	B	I	⁹A					¹⁰O
			²C	O	N	F	U	C	I	U	S
						G					L
⁷C						H					O
³H	O	⁸M	E	O	P	A	T	H	Y		
I		O				⁴N	I	P	P	O	N
N		N				I					
A		O				⁵S	N	O	O	P	Y
		P				T					
		O				A					
		L				⁶N	I	B	B	L	E
		Y									

Multiple Choice Questions

1. Which archaeological site in Punjab takes its name from a village situated near the former course of the Ravi River?
   a) Lothal b) Sumer
   c) Mohenjodaro d) Harappa

2. Name the Man Booker Prize winner who is the author of 'The White Tiger'.
   a) Stephen Hawking b) Arvind Adiga
   c) Alice Munro d) A.S. Byatt

3. Which sport is also known as 'Pugilism'?
   a) Karate b) Badminton
   c) Boxing d) Ice Skating

   The Viceregal Lodge, also known as Rashtrapati Niwas is located on the Observatory Hills of Shimla, Himachal Pradesh. It was formerly the residence of the British Viceroy of India.

4. What theoretical physicist's 1998 book, 'A Brief History of Time' was followed by his 2005 book, 'A Briefer History of Time'?
   a) Stephen Hawking b) Ayn Rand
   c) Michael Lewis d) Ram Charan

5. Name the volcano that destroyed the Roman City of Pompeii in AD 79.
   a) Mt. Etna b) Mt. Pelee
   c) Mt. Vesuvius d) Mt. Helens

6. The functioning of which part of the body is shown by the ECG?

Multiple Choice Questions

    a) Lungs   b) Kidneys
    c) Heart   d) liver

7. How are 'Dried Fennel Seeds' better known in Hindi?
    a) *Hing*   b) *Elaichi*
    c) *Methi*   d) *Saunf*

8. After whom is the international airport in Kolkata named?
    a) Indira Gandhi   b) Vivekananda
    c) Rajiv Gandhi   d) Netaji Subhash Chandra Bose

9. With which sport would you associate the terms: butterfly, breaststroke, freestyle and backstroke?
    a) Shot put   b) Javelin Throw
    c) Long Jump   d) Swimming

10. Which company is popularly known as the 'Big Blue' and is famous for its mainframe technology?
    a) IBM   b) Apple
    c) Google   d) Microsoft

11. Momofuku Ando was the Taiwanese – Japanese businessman who founded the Nissin Food Products Co. Ltd. What is his claim to fame?
    a) Invention of manchurian   b) Invention of instant noodles
    c) Invention of chopsticks   d) Invention of clear soups

12. Which warrior in Indian mythology is believed to have originated the *Chhath Puja Festival* (popular in Bihar) in the honour of the Sun God?
    a) Arjun   b) Karna
    c) Yudhishthira   d) Duryodhana

13. Which of the following city was the capital of Pakistan till 1959?
    a) Islamabad   b) Lahore
    c) Karachi   d) Hyderabad

14. Name the industrialist behind Nano – the 1 lakh rupee car.
    a) Ratan Tata   b) Anand Mahindra
    c) L.N. Mittal   d) Narayan Murthy
15. Name the Indian city that means, 'City of God' in Persian.
    a) Amritsar   b) Allahabad
    c) Kanpur   d) Haridwar
16. Who among the following is married to film producer and director, Kiran Rao?
    a) Shah Rukh Khan   b) Aamir Khan
    c) Salman Khan   d) Saif Ali Khan
17. In which of the following Indian city resides the Silicon Valley of India?
    a) Delhi   b) Mumbai
    c) Chennai   d) Bengaluru

Muhammad Ali had a highly unorthodox boxing style for a heavyweight,

18. Which software company was founded by Bill Gates along with Paul Allen in 1975?
    a) Microsoft   b) Yahoo!
    c) Google   d) Adobe
19. With which would you associate the terms: Walking/Travelling, Slam Dunk and Fast Break?
    a) Basketball   b) Football
    c) Volleyball   d) Cricket
20. Th e city is famous for its scissors, handloom clothes, gold jewellery, sports goods (especially cricket goods), *Gazak* and *Rewri*; and is sometimes called the *city of scissors* or the *sports capital of India*. Identify the city. Th e year, 1857 has a long lasting relationship with this city.
    a) Kanpur   b) Jaipur
    c) Lucknow   d) Meerut

Multiple Choice Questions

21. Name the metallic element that derives its symbol from the Latin word, *natrium* or *natrun*.
    a) Neon
    b) Nitrogen
    c) Sodium
    d) Mercury

22. In which movie series would you come across a computer programmer, 'Neo' who is drawn into a rebellion against the machines?
    a) X-men
    b) Terminator
    c) Transformers
    d) Matrix

23. Which country has *Taka* as its currency?
    a) Bhutan
    b) Bangladesh
    c) Indonesia
    d) Sri Lanka

24. Name the Afghani conqueror who is known for issuing the first *Rupiya* that was in use till the 20th century and is also famously remembered for killing a fully-grown tiger with his bare hands in the Indian jungle.
    a) Humayun
    b) Jahangir
    c) Babur
    d) Sher Shah Suri

25. It served as the capital of the Mughals until 1857, when Mughal emperor Bahadur Shah Zafar was exiled by the British Indian government. It was designated a UNESCO World Heritage Site in 2007. Identify.
    a) Mehrangarh Fort
    b) Golconda Fort
    c) Red Fort
    d) Hawa Mahal

26. Which Mughal emperor derives its name from the Persian word meaning, 'Conqueror of the World'?
    a) Shah Jahan
    b) Akbar
    c) Jahangir
    d) Humayun

27. Name the reform movement that was founded by Swami Dayananda in 1875.

a) Brahmo Samaj b) Arya Samaj
c) Shantiniketan d) Quit India Movement

28. Name the Viceroy who was responsible for the decision of the Partition of Bengal announced on July 19, 1905.

   a) Lord Mountbatten b) Lord Curzon
   c) Lord Adam d) Lord Cornwallis

29. He is revered as the *AdiKavi*, which means *the First Poet*, for he discovered the first *shloka*, i.e., the first verse, which set the base and defined the form to Sanskrit poetry. He is the author of a famous Indian epic. Identify him.

   a) Ved Vyas b) Valmiki
   c) Kabir d) Asvaghosa

30. Constructed from oxidising and weathered ferruginous sandstone by King Narasimhadeva I of the Eastern Ganga Dynasty, this temple in Orissa (Odisha) is one of the most well-renowned temples in India and is a World Heritage Site. Name the temple.

   a) Jagannath Temple b) Lingaraj Temple
   c) Konark Sun Temple d) Rajarani Temple

31. Which Indian deity rides a crow as a *vahana*?

   a) Brahma b) Shani
   c) Kartikeya d) Indra

There are various theories regarding the purpose for which Charminar was constructed. However, it is widely accepted that Charminar was built at the centre of the city, to commemorate the eradication of 'plague', as Muhammad Quli Qutub Shah had prayed for the end of a plague that was ravaging his city and vowed to build a Mosque at the very place where he prayed.

32. According to religious practices of this community, the dead bodies cannot be buried or burnt because the corpses could pollute the *Panchabhootam* (earth, water, air, ether and fire). Hence, their bodies are left in a high-rise, 'Tower of Silence' to be consumed by the scavengers. Identify the community.

Multiple Choice Questions

a) Jains b) Buddhists
c) Parsis d) Muslims

33. What Arabic term meaning, 'pure' was used during the Muslim rule in India for crown lands administered directly by the king without the mediation of *jagirdars* or *mansabdars*? It subsequently acquired a religious connotation – 'pure' referring to the 'people directly under the lord' without any further division of mankind into any other religious fold.

a) Prophet b) Khalsa
c) Adi Granth d) Gurbani

34. Name the Hindu God who is believed to be cursed by Brahmarishi Bhrigu that no person on Earth would ever invoke him or worship him again.

a) Brahma b) Vishnu
c) Shiva d) Indra

35. Name the archaeological site in the Punjab province of Pakistan that is reputed to derive its name from the son of Bharata (the brother of Rama) and Mandavi. During the reign of Chandragupta's grandson Aśoka, it became a great Buddhist centre of learning.

a) Taxila b) Kalinga
c) Harappa d) Mohenjodaro

36. Surrounded by rocky, sandy and five salt ranges, this city located in a Jaisalmer district in the Indian state which means, 'the place of five mirages'. Dr. APJ Abdul Kalam has a special connection with this place. Name the city.

a) Fatehgarh b) Jaisalmer
c) Pokharan d) Jaipur

37. Name the Indian Prime Minister who laid down the five principles called the *Panchsheel* which form the basis of the Non-Aligned Movement (NAM).

a) Lal Bahadur Shastri b) Indira Gandhi
c) Morarji Desai d) Jawaharlal Nehru

38. Who was the chief disciple of the 19th century mystic, Sri Ramakrishna Paramahamsa and is best known for his inspiring speech beginning with "sisters and brothers of America"
    a) Raja Ram Mohan Roy   b) Swami Dayanand Saraswati
    c) Swami Vivekananda   d) Bipin Chandra Pal
39. Name the politician from the Congress party who was the Chief Minister of Madhya Pradesh when the Bhopal Gas Tragedy took place.
    a) Karan Singh   b) Veer Bhadra Singh
    c) Arjun Singh   d) Digvijay Singh
40. Name the national parliament of Denmark that literally means 'People's Th ing'—that is, the people's governing assembly.
    a) Duma   b) Folketin
    c) Congress   d) Bundestag
41. Name the politician who was charged with corruption in the *Taj Corridor* case to upgrade tourist facilities near the Taj Mahal.
    a) Kalyan Singh   b) Mayawati
    c) Mulayam Singh   d) Amar Singh
42. Name the Minister of State in the Ministry of Communications and Technology who is currently an MP from Ajmer constituency.
    a) Milind Deora   b) Rahul Gandhi
    c) Omar Abdullah   d) Sachin Pilot

43. Th e Secretariat of which organisation is in Kathmandu? It was established on December 8, 1985 at Dhaka.
    a) WHO   b) UN
    c) SAARC   d) UNDP

Multiple Choice Questions

44. Who was appointed as the Secretary of State in Barack Obama's government?
    a) Condoleeza Rice   b) Joe Biden
    c) Hillary Clinton   d) Ben Jackson

45. Until 1950, it was known as the 'Viceroy's House' and served as the residence of the Governor-General of India. Which building is being talked about?
    a) The Supreme Court of India   b) The Rashtrapati Bhavan
    c) The High Court of India   d) Parliament House

46. The President of which country married Carla Bruni on February 2, 2008 who is the heiress to the fortune created by the Italian tire manufacturing company, CEAT?
    a) Japan   b) South Korea
    c) France   d) United States of America

47. Who among the following is the ex-officio Chairman of the Rajya Sabha?
    a) The President of India
    b) The Vice-President of India
    c) The Prime Minister of India
    d) The Home Minister of India

48. Name the American President who is the author of the books - *My Life and Giving and How Each of Us Can Change the World*.
    a) George Bush   b) Barack Obama
    c) John Kennedy   d) Bill Clinton

49. Who was the Chief Minister of Uttar Pradesh during the communal riots of 1992 in Ayodhya?
    a) Kalyan Singh   b) Rajnath Singh
    c) Arjun Singh   d) Amar Singh

50. The first Non-Congress government rose to power at the end of the national emergency, but lasted only to give power back to the Congress in 1980. Who headed this government and who was the next Congress PM?
   a) Charan Singh , Indira Gandhi
   b) Morarji Desai, Indira Gandhi
   c) Indira Gandhi, P.V. Narasimha Rao
   d) Morarji Desai, Charan Singh

51. 'Th e Daughter of Destiny' was published in 1988 when she was made the Prime Minister. Her father also had works published during his time like, 'Th e Great Tragedy' and 'If I Am Assassinated'. Which politician is being talked about?
   a) Hilary Clinton   b) Chandrika Kumaratunga
   c) Pratibha Patil   d) Benazir Bhutto

52. Who was born on August 11, 1943 in Neharwali Haveli situated in Daryaganj in Delhi, British India, and stems from a family of government servants?
   a) Benazir Bhutto   b) Mohammad Ali Jinnah
   c) Pervez Musharraf   d) Zulfikar Ali Bhutto

53. Name the American President who resigned because of the Watergate scandal.
   a) George Bush   b) Richard Nixon
   c) Bill Clinton   d) Ronald Reagan

54. In Marathi, it is *Velchi or Veldodaa*. In Malayalam, it is *Aelam*. In Telugu and Tamil, it is *elakkai* and in Kannada it is yelakki. How do we know it popularly in English?
   a) Cardamom   b) Cinnamon
   c) Clove   d) Saffron

The Manhattan Project was a research and development project that produced with the support of the United Kingdom and Canada.

55. What is the term for a partially frozen, often fruity drink and usually a mixture of ingredients served over a mound of crushed ice?

   a) Café Mocha   b) Frappe
   c) Espresso   d) Cappuccino

56. Name the national fish of Bangladesh that can be cooked in more than 50 ways.

   a) Tuna   b) Hilsa
   c) Pomfret   d) Quillfish

57. How do we better know sweet Fried Cottage Cheese Dumplings?

   a) Rasagulla   b) Gulab Jamun
   c) Jalebi   d) Raj Bhog

58. What is the name of the traditional Italian rice dish cooked with broth and flavoured with Parmesan cheese? The name of the dish means literally, 'little rice', and it is one of the most common ways of cooking rice in Italy.

   a) Gimbap   b) Horchata
   c) Kateh   d) Risotto

59. The first restaurant of this fast-food chain was opened by brothers, Richard and Maurice in California in 1940. Their introduction of the 'Speedee Service System' in 1948 established the principles of the modern fast-food restaurant. Identify.

   a) McDonald's   b) Pizza Hut
   c) Domino's Pizza d) Burger King

60. This term is a French language/phrase meaning 'according to the menu', and used in restaurant terminology as: A reference to a menu of items priced and ordered separately, in contrast to a *table d'hôte*. Identify the term.

   a) Cuisine   b) À la carte
   c) Culinary   d) Saute

61. During the Edo period, it was referred to as *pickled fish conserved in vinegar*. Nowadays, it can be defined as a dish containing rice which has been prepared with vinegar. Identify.

   a) Sashimi b) Wasabi
   c) Gyudon   d) Sushi

62. Who is the host of *Khana Khazana* – a popular cookery programme shown on the Zee TV every Sunday, since 1993?

   a) Vikas Khanna b) Sanjeev Kapoor
   c) Hari Nayak   d) Prasad Nayak

63. The story of this popular Indian dish's origin lies with a man named Kundanlal Gujral, who ran a restaurant called Moti Mahal in Peshawar before the partition of British India. This dish at the Moti Mahal so impressed the first Prime Minister of India, Pt. Jawaharlal Nehru, that he made it a regular at official banquets. Identify the Indian dish.

   a) Dal Makhani   b) Tandoori Chicken
   c) Paneer Pasanda d) Katti Rolls

64. The English name for these are derived the from Latin word meaning, 'nail' as the buds vaguely resemble small irregular nails in shape. These are used as a spice in cuisines all over the world and are a native of Indonesia. What am I talking about?

   a) Cardamom b) Cinnamon
   c) Clove   d) Saffron

65. What name is given to a person, usually a coffee-house employee, who prepares and serves espresso-based coffee drinks?

   a) Mocha b) Barista
   c) Costa d) Espresso

66. What originated in Italy as the Neapolitan pie with tomato?

   a) Pasta b) Macaroni
   c) Pizza d) Burger

Multiple Choice Questions

Excalibur is the legendary sword of King Arthur, sometimes attributed with magical powers or associated with the rightful sovereignty of Great Britain.

67. Her first book, 'Th e Pleasures of Vegetarian Cooking', which was published in 1974, was an instant success with Indian housewives. She has been awarded the *Padma Shri* on Jan 26, 2007 by the President of India towards her contributions in the field of cookery. Who is she?

    a) Julie Sahney b) Madhur Jaffery
    c) Savita Mehta d) Tarla Dalal

68. Name the Indian film personality who started Excel Entertainment Pvt. Ltd. along with Ritesh Sidhwani.

    a) Karan Johar b) Aditya Chopra
    c) Nitin Mukesh d) Farhan Akhtar

69. Who was the eldest child of actress Shobhana Samarth who started her career as an actress as a fourteen-year-old in *Hamari Beti* (1950)?

    a) Nutan b) Tanuja
    c) Madhubala d) Nargis

70. Which movie was directed by Danny Boyle and co-directed in India by Loveleen Tandan? It is an adaptation of the novel, Q & A by Indian author and diplomat Vikas Swarup.

    a) Chak De b) Slumdog Millionaire
    c) Iqbal d) The Namesake

71. Which American vocal group is named after a flea market in Orlando, Florida and had its performance at the Sea World, Orlando in May 1993?

    a) The Beatles b) Boyzone
    c) U2 d) Backstreet Boys

72. Which movie's tagline was 'Nothing on earth could come between them'?

    a) Matrix b) Titanic

c) The Curious Case of Benjamin Button
d) Angels & Demons

73. Name the company joined as an intern by Ranbir Kapoor in the movie, 'Rocket Singh: Salesman of the Year'.
    a) AYS   b) ATS
    c) AMC   d) ABC

74. Name the Bollywood director who owns a stake in the NDTV Imagine.
    a) Farhan Akhtar   b) Raju Hirani
    c) Vidu Vinod Chopra   d) Karan Johar

75. Who played the role of James bond in the 22nd James Bond film, 'Quantum of Solace'?
    a) Sean Connery   b) Roger Moore
    c) Pierce Brosnan d) Daniel Craig

76. Enrique Martín Morales is a Puerto Ricanpop singer and actor who achieved prominence, first as a member of the Latinboy band, Menudo, and then as a solo artist after 1991. How do we better know him?
    a) Enrique Iglesias   b) Ricky Martin
    c) Eros Ramazzotti   d) Daddy Yankee

77. "This is the first time that the *Singapore Airlines* has purchased the rights of an *Indian movie*. The film will be screened on all its international flights from December 1," Airlines manager, southern India, Bharat Mahadevan told reporters. Which movie's rights starring Tamil superstar Rajnikanth were purchased?
    a) Raghupathi Raghava Rajaramb) Veera
    c) Sivaji-The Boss   d) Blood Stone

78. Name the veteran theatre actor, who is best known for his role as *Mohammad Ali Jinnah* in *Gandhi*.
    a) Om Puri   b) Satish Shah
    c) Alyqu Padamsee   d) Javed Akhtar

79. Konkana Sen Sharma used to work for which magazine in the movie, *Wake Up Sid*?
    a) Mumbai Beat
    b) Mumbai Rains
    c) Mumbai
    d) Love Mumbai

80. In which Indian city, would you find the largest film studio complex in the world?
    a) Bengaluru
    b) Mumbai
    c) Chennai
    d) Hyderabad

81. Priyanka Chopra played the role of a staff of which fashion magazine in the film, *Dostana*?
    a) Femina
    b) Esquire
    c) Verve
    d) Chanel

82. Which of the following words appear on the logo of Doordarshan?
    a) Satyameva Jayate
    b) Satyam Shivam Sundaram
    c) Jai Hind
    d) Jai Bharat

83. Which form of medicine was first proposed by German physician Samuel Hahnemann in 1796 that attempts to treat patients with heavily diluted preparations?
    a) Ayurveda
    b) Unani
    c) Siddha
    d) Homeopathy

84. Which chemical element's name was made from an English word that originally meant an alkali extracted in a pot from the ash of burnt wood or tree leaves?
    a) Phosphorus
    b) Pentium
    c) Potassium
    d) Palladium

85. Which chemical element is extracted by mainly two processes: the *Sicilian process* and the *Frasch process*?
    a) Potassium
    b) Sodium
    c) Aluminium
    d) Sulphur

86. They were discovered by accident by a scientist named, Wilhelm Röentgen in 1895, while using Cathode ray tubes and were given the current name, since nobody knew what they were or what they were made of at that time! Identify.
    a) Alpha Rays
    b) Beta Rays
    c) Gamma Rays
    d) X-Rays

87. Which scientific term is used to describe the change in direction of a wave due to a change in its speed?
    a) Reflection
    b) Refraction
    c) Dispersion
    d) Interference

88. Which substance is used for the preservation of biological specimens?
    a) Formalin
    b) Sulphuric Acid
    c) Nitric Acid
    d) Hydrochloric Acid

89. Which of the following type of mirror is used for shaving?
    a) Convex Mirror
    b) Horizontal Mirror
    c) Concave Mirror
    d) Vertical Mirror

90. Which of the following gases is also known as *Rotten Eggs Gas* because of its characteristic foul odour of rotten eggs?
    a) Nitrous Oxide
    b) Ammonium Nitrate
    c) Hydrogen Sulphide
    d) Calcium Acetate

91. Which of the following is the base solvent used in nail polish remover?
    a) Citric Acid
    b) Ammonia
    c) Acetone
    d) Sodium Hydroxide

92. Which of the following is the SI unit of capacitance?
    a) Coulomb
    b) Farad

c) Ampere d) Volt

The Golconda Fort, popularly known in Telugu as 'Golla Konda', means 'Shepherd's Hill'.

93. Name the *avatar* of Vishnu that appears in the *Vedas* and the *Puranas* as the *physician of the Gods* and the *God of Ayurvedic medicine*.
    a) Vamana b) Dhanvantari
    c) Kalki d) Parashurama

94. Who is the author of the books: *Dialogue Concerning the Two Chief World Systems* and *Sidereus Nuncius*, or Th Sidereal Messenger*?
    a) Isaac Newton b) Galileo Galilei
    c) Nikola Tesla d) James Henry

95. Which of the following organs stores bile produced by the liver?
    a) Small Intestine b) Gall Bladder
    c) Stomach d) Heart

96. He and Edison became adversaries in part because of Edison's promotion of Direct Current (DC) for electric power distribution over the more efficient alternating current advocated by him and Westinghouse in the late 1880s. Who is he?
    a) Isaac Newton b) Galileo Galilei
    c) Nikola Tesla d) James Henry

97. Which card game derives its name from a French word meaning 'Patience'?
    a) Hearts b) Free Cell
    c) Solitaire d) Rummy

98. Which game owes its origin to a Canadian-born physical education professor and instructor, Dr. James Naismith, who was trying to keep his gym class active on a rainy day sought a vigorous indoor game to keep his students occupied and at proper levels of fitness?

a) Badminton b) Basketball
c) Throwball d) Volleyball

99. In which game would you come across the following defensive strokes: Push, Chop, Block, Push-Block, Kill Spin, Side Drive, Lob and Drop Shoy?

   a) Badminton b) Volleyball
   c) Table Tennis d) Baseball

100. What is the height of a basketball ring from the ground in the game of basketball?

   a) 8 feet b) 10 feet
   c) 12 feet d) 14 feet

101. This game originated as a sport in Britain during the 1800s, where it was played amongst the upper-class as an after dinner entertainment activity. The sound generated in the play gave the game its first nicknames of 'Wiff-waff' and 'Ping-pong'. Identify the game.

   a) Table Tennis b) Badminton
   c) Basketball d) Lawn Tennis

102. Which cable television network was originally conceived by Bill Rasmussen, a television sports reporter and had Sports Center as its flagship programme?

   a) Star Sports b) Neo Sports
   c) ZEE Sports d) ESPN

103. Who is the current manager of the Argentine National Team?

   a) Pele b) AlfioBasile
   c) Diego Maradona d) Daniel Passarella

104. The motto of which sporting event is Citius, Altius, Fortius, a Latin expression meaning 'Faster, Higher, Stronger'?

   a) Olympics b) Asian Games
   c) Commonwealth Games d) Afro-Asian Games

105. With which sport would you associate the terms: Walking/Travelling, Slam Dunk and Fast Break?

a) Football b) Basketball
c) Baseball d) Throwball

 Madan Mohan Malviya. It is one of the largest residential universities in Asia, with over 20,000 students.

106. Th e game was played widely in ancient India by the name of *Moksha Patamu*. Moksha Patamu was perhaps invented by Hindu spiritual teachers to teach children about the effects of good deeds as opposed to bad deeds. It made its way to England, and was eventually introduced in the United States of America by game-pioneer Milton Bradley in 1943. Identify the game.

a) Ludo b) Monopoly
c) Snakes & Ladders d) Scrabble

107. Who began his career as a commentator at the age of 19 with the All India Radio, while living in Hyderabad and was the first Indian commentator to be invited by the Australian Broadcasting Corporation during India's cricket series before the 1992 Cricket World Cup?

a) Ravi Shastri b) Harsha Bhogle
c) Ian Chappell d) Navjot Singh Sidhu

108. Who was the first cricketer to score a Test century for the Indian cricket team, which he achieved on debut?

a) Lala Amarnath b) Kapil Dev
c) Sunil Gavaskar d) Sachin Tendulkar

109. Name the Indian shooter who won the silver medal in Men's Double Trap at the 2004 Summer Olympics in Athens.

a) Rajyavardhan Singh Rathore b) Abhinav Bhindra
c) Jaspal Rana d) Randhir Singh

110. Name the Oscar-winning film director, who is the artistic director of the opening ceremony of London 2012 Olympic Games.

a) Shekhar Kapoor b) Danny Boyle
c) Steven Spielberg d) Ashutosh Gowarikar

111. Name the mascot for the 1982 Asian Games after whom an amusement park in Delhi was named.

a) Shera b) Ranga
c) Appu d) Bhola

112. Which famous social networking site was created by Mark Zuckerberg? In 2008, Collins English Dictionary declared it as their new *Word of the Year*.

a) LinkedIn b) Facebook
c) Orkut, d) Wayne

113. Which programming language was initially called 'Oak' after an oak tree that stood outside the developer's office?

a) C b) Logo
c) Java d) Basic

114. What term is used to describe a person who spends plenty of time on the internet?

a) Netphile b) Netizen
c) Cybernaut d) Cyberphile

115. Which company was the first to distribute mouse as a standard component with the personal computer?

a) Apple computers b) IBM
c) HP d) Compaq

116. He started his career with a small stint at the Apple and then the *Firepower Systems Inc.* which he left to co-found *HoTMaiL* (Hot Mail, written such as upper-case letters form HTML) with Jack Smith. In 2008, he launched his latest venture *SabSeBolo.com*, a free web-based tele-conferencing system. His future plans include developing a new city in India called 'Nanocity'. Identify the person in question.

a) AzimPremji b) Sabeer Bhatia

Multiple Choice Questions

c) Vinod Khosla   d) Narayan Murthy

117. This law describes a long-term trend in the history of computing hardware, in which the number of transistors that can be placed inexpensively on an integrated circuit has doubled approximately, every two years. Which law is being described above?

   a) Murphy's Law   b) Moore's Law
   c) Peter's Law   d) Parkinson's Law

that surround the dome at its base, making it appear as a budding rose) is the mausoleum of Mohammed Adil Shah, Sultan of Bijapur.

118. Methods for uniquely recognising humans based upon one or more intrinsic physical or behavioural traits like *fingerprints, iris scan, voice, face recognition* is known as what?

   a) Biotronics   b) Mechatronics
   c) Biometrics   d) Biomechanics

119. In 1959, the invention of which product by Robert Noyce made the size of the electronic products to shirk and become smaller?

   a) Silicon   b) Transistors
   c) Resistors   d) Integrated Circuits

120. In Japan, the series was released as *Over Drivin* and was originally developed by the Canadian based company *Distinctive Software*, which became known as EA *Canada*. Identify the series.

   a) NFS   b) Max Payne
   c) Age of Empires   d) Mario

121. Th e company was formed by Rod Canion, Jim Harris and Bill Murto — former Texas Instruments senior managers and derived its name from Compatibilty and Quality. Name the company.

   a) Yahoo   b) Microsoft

c) Cisco d) COMPAQ

122. Karan Thapar: Let me start with a simple question. It is said that 80 per cent of Indians have Election Commission identity cards, others have ration cards, some people have BPL cards, others have driving licence and passports, there are even PAN cards. Why on top of this do we need a Unique Identification Number?

    Who is being interviewed?

    a) Nandan Nilekani   b) Narayan Murthy
    c) Azim Premji   d) S. Ramadorai

123. Name the businessman whose father owned the Western India Vegetable Product Company which made hydrogenated vegetable oils and fats.

    a) Narayan Murthy   b) Azim Premji
    c) Subroto Baghchi   d) Rajesh Hukku

124. My lasting tagline has been 'Business is our middle name'. Who am I?

    a) IBM   b) Sony
    c) Sanyo   d) Dell

125. What do you call software that has been released to users for software testing before its official release?

    a) Alpha   b) Beta
    c) Gamma   d) Theta

126. The Indian version of *Google Earth* and Wikimapia was launched on August 12, the 90th birth anniversary of Vikram Sarabhai. It means 'earth' in Sanskrit. It's name is inspired from a movie character. Name the project.

    a) Bhuvan   b) Bhumi
    c) Bhudan   d) Bhushan

127. Meaning weight in Spanish, it was the name given to the *8-real coin in Spain* and particularly in Spanish America. Identify.

a) Dollar b) Euro
c) Peso d) Dinar

128. Known in Thai as *Krung Thep Mahanakhon* meaning, 'City of angels' for short, it was a small trading post at the mouth of the Chao Phraya River during the Ayutthaya Kingdom. Identify the city.
   a) Pattaya b) Bangkok
   c) Phuket d) Lampang

129. Which Mughal emperor's poems were compiled into the Kulliyyat-i Zafar?
   a) Aurangzeb b) Bahadur Shah Zafar
   c) Shah Jahan d) Babur

Playing cards were invented in Imperial China. They were found in China as

130. Which country was the first time finalist in FIFA 2010 World Cup?
   a) Italy b) Brazil
   c) Argentina d) Spain

131. Which of the following family name was a title used for people who used to maintain the accounts and records of the villages and used to collect taxes?
   a) Bhide b) Kulkarni
   c) Manjarekar d) Bhagwat

132. American President *Woodrow Wilson* was awarded the Nobel Peace Prize *in 1919* for the foundation of which organisation?
   a) Red Cross b) United Nations
   c) SAARC d) The League of Nations

133. In which Indian city would you be if you are travelling via Rajiv Gandhi Sea Link?
   a) Delhi b) Kolkata
   c) Chennai d) Mumbai

134. Which political party's mouthpiece is named 'Saamna'?
    a) Shiv Sena   b) TMC
    c) SP   d) BJP

135. Who among the following was not a *Navaratna* in the court of Akbar?
    a) Abul Fazl   b) Birbal
    c) Tansen   d) Kalidas

136. Which of the following languages does not use, 'Devanagari' as their script?
    a) Hindi   b) Nepali
    c) Gujarati   d) Marathi

137. Which of the following business house was behind the foundation of the industrial city, 'Jamshedpur'?
    a) Tatas   b) Birlas
    c) Ambanis   d) Goenkas

138. Which political party was founded at Dhaka, Bangladesh in 1906? Sir Aga Khan was the first Honorary President of this party.
    a) Muslim League   b) Indian National Congress
    c) Akali Dal   d) National Conference

139. Who was the host of the popular TV serial, *Surabhi* along with Siddharth Kak that was telecasted on Doordarshan?
    a) Divya Dutta   b) Pallavi Joshi
    c) Renuka Shahane   d) Durga Jasraj

140. Which brand was the main sponsor of the first incarnation of the weekly radio countdown show hosted by Ameen Sayani?
    a) Cibaca   b) Binaca
    c) Colgate   d) Pepsodent

141. Name the American sitcom that had the following main cast

members: Jennifer Aniston, Courteney Cox Arquette, Lisa Kudrow, Matt LeBlanc, Matthew Perry and David Schwimmer.

a) I Love Lucy
b) Friends
c) I Dream of Jeannie
d) The Simpsons

142. Which of the following is the STD code of Bangalore (Bengaluru)?

a) 078
b) 079
c) 080
d) 081

143. According to the Hindu mythology, the area around this city was ruled by a demon, Mahishasura. The city is famous for the festivities that take place during the Dussehra festival when the city receives a large number of tourists. Name the Indian city.

a) Mathura
b) Mysore
c) Manesar
d) Mangalore

Popular tradition dates the founding of the MCC to 1787 when Thomas Lord opened the ground he bought on the site now occupied by Dorset Square which the club adopted as its home venue.

144. Which British children's author is most widely known for the character, 'Noddy'? Her first book, *Child Whispers*, a collection of poems was published in 1922.

a) JK Rowling
b) Enid Blyton
c) Sidney Sheldon
d) Anita Desai

145. Each bank note has its amount written in how many languages illustrating the diversity of the country?

a) 15
b) 17
c) 19
d) 22

146. This Indian festival literally means, 'boiling over' which refers to rice cooked in milk and jaggery. Identify the festival.

a) Pongal
b) Onam
c) Muharram
d) Bihu

147. Name the American rock band that had the following earlier names: *Xero* and *Hybrid Theory*

a) Bon Jovi b) AeroSmith
c) Nirvana d) Linkin Park

148. Whose secret identity is Bruce Wayne, a wealthy businessman who lives in Gotham City?

a) Superman b) Spiderman
c) Batman d) Phantom

149. In which Indian state would you be if you are visiting Rohtang Pass that connects the Kullu Valley with the Lahaul and Spiti Valleys of Himachal Pradesh?

a) Himachal Pradesh b) Jammu and Kashmir
c) Uttarakhand d) Uttar Pradesh

150. Which monthly magazine was started in January 1993 in Allahabad by Amit Saigal and Shena Gamat Saigal after they realised the lack of support system for the Indian rock musicians?

a) The Music Magazine b) Rock Street Journal
c) Shruti d) Rolling Stones India

151. The motorbike and four-wheeled automobile were invented in this German town and it is sometimes referred to as, 'The cradle of the automobile'. Identify the German city.

a) Berlin b) Munich
c) Frankfurt d) Stuttgart

152. Which of the following means "awakened one" or "the enlightened one"?

a) Buddha b) Mahavira
c) Rama d) Krishna

153. Which city houses the headquarters of the International Cricket Council (ICC)?

a) England b) Dubai
c) New York d) Melbourne

154. Launched on July 7, 1984, it had an average viewership of 50 million per episode. In a research paper, Arvind Singhal and Evertt M Rogers say even in non-Hindi speaking regions, the

soap's rating was between 20 and 40%, while in north India, it ranged between 60 and 90%. Veteran actor, Ashok Kumar, who delivered an epilogue at the end of each episode, got nearly 4,00,000 letters in response. Which soap was it?

a) Circus
b) Fauji
c) Hum Log
d) Buniyaad

155. Which detergent brand, launched in 1949 as 'America's Washday favourite', gets its name from the term for the cyclic rise and fall of the earth's ocean surface?

a) Tide
b) Ariel
c) Surf Excel
d) Rin

156. Name the Nobel laureate who was an ambulance driver for the American Red Cross during WWI.

a) TS Eliot
b) WB Yeats
c) Ernest Hemmingway
d) William Shakespeare

Secretary of State Pietro Gasparri, on behalf of Pope Pius XI and by Prime Minister Benito Mussolini on behalf of King Victor Emmanuel III of Italy.

157. Who was the first Indian to win 'Miss World' title?

a) Sushmita Sen
b) Aishwarya Rai
c) Lara Dutta
d) Reita Faria

158. Who is called the *father of computing* for his contributions to the basic design of the computer through what he called the *analytical engine*?

a) Alan Turing
b) Charles Babbage
c) RD Henderson
d) John McCarthy

159. Who was awarded the *2006 Nobel Peace Prize*, along with *Grameen Bank*, for efforts to create economic and social development through micro-credit?

a) Amartya Sen
b) Muhammad Yunus
c) Meghnad Desai
d) C Rangarajan

160. In 1976, Hayes Noel, Bob Gurnsey, and Charles Gaines were chatting about Gaines' recent trip to Africa and his experiences hunting buffalo. Eager to recreate the adrenaline rush that came with the thrill of the hunt, and inspired by Richard Connell's, *The Most Dangerous Game*, the two friends came up with the idea to create a game. Which game did they create?

   a) Badminton   b) Throw Ball
   c) Paintball   d) Basketball

161. Keith Richards was the lead guitarist of which English Rock band formed in April 1962?

   a) Pink Floyd   b) The Beatles
   c) The Rolling Stones   d) Led Zepplin

162. He was the interim Prime Minister of India twice for thirteen days each. The first time after the death of Prime Minister Jawaharlal Nehru in 1964, and the second time after the death of Prime Minister Lal Bahadur Shastri in 1966. Who is he?

   a) GulzariLal Nanda   b) IK Gujral
   c) PV Narasimha Rao   d) Indira Gandhi

163. Which American President went to Paris in 1919 to create the *League of Nations* and shape the *Treaty of Versailles*?

   a) Richard Nixon   b) D. Eisenhower
   c) John Keneddy   d) Woodrow Wilson

164. Which word began as a West Coast slang term and was first used to refer to music in Chicago in about 1915?

   a) Pop   b) Jazz
   c) Karaoke   d) Sufi

165. Which Indian founder and present Chief Mentor started out his career at *Patni Computer Systems*?

   a) Subroto Bagchi   b) KS Kapoor
   c) Azim Premji   d) Narayan Murthy

Multiple Choice Questions

166. The airport that serves Venice is named after which famous explorer and traveller who lived in the city?
    a) Marco Polo   b) Ibn Battuta
    c) Robert Dessaiz   d) Hiuen Tsang

167. Which of the following organisations is a society, registered under the Tamil Nadu Societies Registration Act? Its logo is derived from the emblem of the *Order of the Star of India*, India's highest order of chivalry during the British Raj and also its *Coat of Arms*.
    a) RBI   b) FICCI
    c) SBI   d) BCCI

168. Released in 2000, Kandisa acquired a cult status and propelled this band into the status of one of India's most original and creative bands. Identify the band.
    a) Parikrama   b) Indian Ocean
    c) Warriors of Peace d) Fossils

Swayamvara of Rukmini, he acted as the messenger between Shishupala and Rukmini's father Bhishmaka, at the request of King Jarasandha. Ultimately, Bhishmaka decided that Rukmini would marry Shishupala, but instead she

Krishna and King Jarasandha's army.

169. Name the noble nominee who used to ask to sell his autograph for Rs 5, which he gave to a fund dedicated to an integral part and icon of the Swadeshi Movement.
    a) JawaharLal Nehru b) Mahatma Gandhi
    c) Sardar Patel   d) Lala Lajpat Rai

170. This former great Pakistani name has got permanently connected to Sunil Gavaskar as his was the only wicket that Gavaskar ever claimed in his career. Name him.
    a) Imran Khan   b) Moin Khan
    c) Zaheer Abbas   d) Shoaib Malik

171. Which structure was erected to commemorate the landing of their Majesties, King George V and Queen Mary at *Apollo*

Bunder, when they visited India in 1911?

a) Victoria Memorial b) Gateway of India
c) Charminar d) Qutub Minar

172. The origins of the name of which character by Walt Disney was said to have been inspired by an Australian cricket legend when he made the news after being dismissed for a score of zero against New York West Indians?

a) Mickey Mouse b) Goofy
c) Donald Duck d) Pinocchio

173. Name the Indian city founded by Raja Suraj Sen who named it after a sage, whose influence almost took him by surprise.

a) Gwalior b) Patna
c) Chandigarh d) Bharatpur

174. The National Science Day is celebrated in India on February 28, each year to mark the discovery of what?

a) Raman effect b) Saha Equation
c) Concept of Zero d) Atomic Bomb

175. The home of which Hindu God is situated on Mount Meru in the Heaven?

a) Kartikeya b) Vishnu
c) Agni d) Indra

176. Which city was founded by *Vanraj Chavda*, the most prominent king of the Chavda Dynasty, in the 8th century? The 2001 award-winning film, *Lagaan* is based in a village in some region of this city.

a) Bikaner b) Khajuraho
c) Champaner d) Tanjore

177. Sansarpur has the rare distinction of having produced the largest number of Olympians from India and hence is known as the 'Mecca of Indian Hockey'. In which Indian state is it located?

a) Haryana b) Punjab
c) Rajasthan d) Madhya Pradesh

178. Who started her career at the age of 14 in the 1950 film, *Hamari Beti*, directed by her mother, Shobhna Samarth?

   a) Hema Malini   b) Rekha
   c) Sharmila Tagore   d) Nutan

179. The name of which Indian state literally means, 'three cities'?

   a) Tripura   b) Meghalaya
   c) Mizoram   d) Manipur

180. Who amongst the following was the founder of the Sikh Empire?

   a) Maharaja Ranjit Singh
   b) Maharaja Surajmal
   c) Maharaja Bhupinder Singh
   d) Maharaja Yadavindra Singh

181. The name of which mathematician is the anglicised version of a Greek name meaning, 'Good Glory'?

   a) Pythagoras   b) Isaac Newton
   c) Rene Descartes   d) Euclid

to use the term, 'magazine,' on the analogy of a military storehouse of varied materials, ultimately derived from the Arabic word, 'makhazin' ('storehouses') in the French language.

182. Which fort was originally referred to as 'Qila-i-Mubarak' (the blessed fort), because it was the residence of the royal family?

   a) Golconda Fort   b) Red Fort
   c) Fort William   d) Mehrangarh Fort

183. The name of which ancient town is derived from the name of the son of Bharata, the brother of the Hindu God, Rama? The name literally means the 'City of Cut Stone'.

a) Pataliputra b) Taxila
c) Ujjain d) Kurukshetra

184. The Beaufort scale is an empirical measure that relates wind speed to the observed conditions at sea or on land. If 10 represent a storm on this scale, what does 12 represent?

   a) Violent storm b) Tsunami
   c) Hurricane d) Cyclone

185. Jobe Charnock was a servant and administrator of the English East India Company, traditionally regarded as the founder of which Indian city?

   a) Delhi b) Mumbai
   c) Kolkata d) Chennai

186. Which *avatar* of Vishnu is most known for ridding the world of Kshatriyas, 21 times over after the mighty king Kartavirya killed his father?

   a) Parashurama b) Narasimha
   c) Vamana d) Balarama

187. She was born probably in 1828 in the holy town of Varanasi into a Brahmin family. She was named *Manikarnika* and was nicknamed *Manu*. How do we popularly know her?

   a) Rani Lakshmi Bai b) Mumtaz
   c) Noor Jahan d) Razia Sultan

188. Name the actress who made her acting debut in the movie, *Sapno Ka Saudagar* (1968).

   a) Hema Malini b) Rekha
   c) Sharmila Tagore d) Nutan

189. Which of the following gases is used for refrigeration?

   a) Argon b) Helium
   c) Hydrogen d) Freon

190. Name the Indian President who founded the *Bihar Law Weekly*.
   a) SD Sharma   b) Zakir Husain
   c) Rajendra Prasad   d) V.V. Giri

191. The earliest known reference to which game is in a 1744 British publication, *A Little Pretty Pocket-Book* by John Newbery?
   a) Basketball   b) Baseball
   c) Badminton   d) Volleyball

192. Who was the founding editor of the famous newspaper, *Kesari*?
   a) Mahatma Gandhi   b) Jawaharlal Nehru
   c) Lokmanya Tilak   d) Muhammad Iqbal

193. Name the person who announced the radical plan offering India the *dominion status* in 1942.
   a) Lord Minto   b) Lord Curzon
   c) Lord Wavell   d) Stafford Cripps

194. The characters that make up this country's name mean, 'sun-origin'. Identify the country.
   a) China   b) Tibet
   c) Japan   d) Malaysia

195. Who is the author of the book, *Dreams From My Father: A story of Race and Inheritance*?
   a) Barack Obama   b) Nelson Mandela
   c) Bill Clinton   d) George Bush

196. Name the film character that climbed up the Empire State Building and the World Trade Centre of USA.
   a) Bruce Lee   b) Jackie Chan
   c) King Kong   d) Batman

197. About 92 percent of the world's diamonds are cut and polished in which Indian city?
   a) Surat
   b) Ahmedabad
   c) Delhi
   d) Mumbai

198. The fans of which football club often refer to themselves as 'Gooners', the name is derived from the team's nickname, 'The Gunners'?
   a) Barcelona
   b) Arsenal
   c) Manchester United
   d) Liverpool

199. Satyajit Ray filmed two of this writer's works – *Sadgati* and *Shatranj Ke Khiladi*. Identify the writer.
   a) Harivanshrai Bachchan
   b) Premchand
   c) Mahadevi Varma
   d) Kaifi Azmi

200. Which of the following is *a country of thousand lakes and islands*—about 188,000 lakes and 179,000 islands?
   a) Finland
   b) Greenland
   c) New Zealand
   d) Melbourne

201. In 1957, who was re-elected to the presidency, becoming the only President to have been elected twice for the office?
   a) Zakir Hussain
   b) Rajendra Prasad
   c) Neelam Reddy
   d) Giani Zail Singh

202. Name the artist who had the capacity of writing with one hand and painting with other simultaneously.
   a) Karl Marx
   b) Renoir
   c) Vincent Van Gogh
   d) Leonardo da Vinci

203. Name the American charged in the Mumbai plot of performing surveillance for the militant group, *Lashkar-e-Taiba*
   a) David Cooper
   b) Mary Whitter

c) David Headley d) Bill Morris

204. Name the Nobel laureate who was responsible for producing the first man-made gene in his laboratory in the early seventies.
   a) Dr. Hargobind Khorana b) Dr. P C Ray
   c) Dr. S K Gupta d) Dr. Harkishan Sinha

205. In the Indian epic, *Ramayana*, who was the son of Aru, a nephew of Garuda? He tried to rescue Sita from Ravana when Ravana was on his way to Lanka after kidnapping Sita.
   a) Sugriva b) Jatayu
   c) Vibhishana d) Indrajit

206. Kalamkari is a type of hand-painted or block-printed cotton textile, produced in parts of India. In which Indian state this art originated?
   a) Bihar b) Tamil Nadu
   c) Odisha d) Andhra Pradesh

207. English poet Alexander Pope was moved by this scientist's accomplishments to write the famous epitaph:

   Nature and nature's laws lay hid in night;

   God said "Let _____ be" and all was light.

   Identify the scientist.
   a) Isaac Newton b) Albert Einstein
   c) Charles Darwin d) Louis Pasteur

208. Ignacio 'Nacho' Anaya was a restaurateur credited as the inventor of *nachos*. What was his nationality?
   a) Mexican b) Italian
   c) French d) Russian

209. Which is the longest, heaviest and by most measures, the strongest bone in the human body?
   a) Patella b) Femur

c) Trapezium   d) Fibula

210. The name of which Indian city is derived from the Sanskrit words meaning, 'one who carries date palm'?

 a) Khajuraho   b) Kanpur
 c) Kannauj   d) Kharagpur

211. In his autobiography, *Mein Kampf*, he described how, in his youth, he wanted to become a painter, but his aspirations were ruined because he failed the entrance exam of the Academy of Fine Arts, Vienna. Who is he?

 a) Benito Mussolini   b) Lenin
 c) Joseph Stalin   d) Adolf Hitler

212. Which sport was invented by Dr. P. Aaron Potter in Swaziland in the late 1890s?

 a) Basketball   b) Baseball
 c) Badminton   d) Volleyball

213. In the mathematical equation, '12-7=5', what is the subtrahend?

 a) 12   b) 7
 c) 5   d) Equal sign

214. Which Indian cricketer's restaurant has an item named 'Multan ke Sultan ki Tikdi' in the menu?

 a) Virendra Sehwag   b) Gautam Gambhir
 c) MS Dhoni   d) Sourav Ganguly

215. As mentioned in the *Mahabharata* epic, which holy city was the capital of the Avanti Kingdom and therefore, is also known as *Avantika*?

 a) Ayodhya   b) Taxila
 c) Ujjain   d) Lumbini

216. Which sportsperson played the role of an underworld character in the movie, *Kabhi Ajnabhi The*, which also featured his contemporary Sandip Patil?

Multiple Choice Questions

a) Kapil Dev b) Lala Amarnath
c) Syed Kirmani d) Ravi Shastri

217. Who amongst the following is known as *Halayudha*?
   a) Balarama b) Hanuman
   c) Karna d) Arjun

218. 'The Road Not Taken' is a poem by which poet, published in 1916 in the collection, *Mountain Interval*?
   a) Robert Frost b) Ernest Hemingway
   c) William Blake d) William Shakespeare

219. Which dance form was the result of the *Bhakti Movement* in the 16th century?
   a) Kuchipudi b) Bihu
   c) Kathak d) Bharatanatyam

220. Which author wrote her first book, *The Rabbit* at the age of six?
   a) J.K. Rowling b) Enid Blyton
   c) Arundhati Roy d) VS Naipaul

221. Who is the only Indian to win both the *Nishan-e-Pakistan* and the *Bharat Ratna*?
   a) Morarji Desai b) Jawaharlal Nehru
   c) Dilip Kumar d) JRD Tata

222. Which chemical element shares its name with Superman's home planet?
   a) Neon b) Xenon
   c) Krypton d) Argon

223. During the reigns of which ruler did Ibn Batuta visit India?
   a) Iltutmish b) Ala-ud-din-Khilji
   c) Balban d) Muhammad Bin Tughlaq

224. Who said, 'I regard India as my Motherland and my Goddess, the people in India are my kith and kin, and loyal and steadfast work for their political and social emancipation is my highest religion and duty'?

a) Gopal Krishna Gokhale b) Bal Gangadhar Tilak
c) Bipin Chandra Pal d) Lala Lajpat Rai

225. Who drew up the territorial borders dividing India and Pakistan?

a) General Alanbrooke, b) Philip Mason
c) Major Radcliffe d) Major Rees

226. The attack on Pearl Harbour was a surprise military strike conducted by the Imperial Japanese Navy against the United States naval base at Pearl Harbour on the morning of December 7, 1941. In which state is Pearl Harbour?

a) Alaska b) Bahamas
c) Hawaii d) Philippines

227. *Pithora* is a highly ritualistic painting done on the walls by several tribes like *Rathwas*, *Bhilals* and *Naykas*, in a village called Tejgadh. Identify the state associated with the art.

a) Gujarat b) Punjab
c) Madhya Pradesh d) Odisha

228. The United Nations Headquarters resides in the international territory of which city?

a) Vienna b) New York
c) Geneva d) Nairobi

229. Which of the following is the world's *highest uninterrupted waterfall*, with a height of 979 m (3,212 ft) and a plunge of 807 m (2,648 ft)?

a) Niagra Falls b) Angel Falls
c) Tugela Falls d) Rhine Falls

230. *La Tomatinais*, a festival in which the participants get involved in *tomato fight* purely for fun and is held on the last Wednesday of August, during the week of festivities of Buñol. In which country is it held?

a) Spain b) Germany
c) France d) Switzerland

Multiple Choice Questions

231. Which of the following is known worldwide as *'the heart of the American theatre industry'*?
    a) Madison Avenue
    b) Broadway
    c) Baker Street
    d) Lombard Street

232. Which of the following denim companies produce the '501' line of jeans?
    a) Calvin Klein
    b) Pepe
    c) Spykar
    d) Levi Strauss

233. Which of the following is the seat of the President of Germany, whose official residence is *Schloss Bellevue*?
    a) Frankfurt
    b) Munich
    c) Brussels
    d) Berlin

234. In 1863, what did Abraham Lincoln declare a national holiday in *orderto foster,* a sense of American unity between the Northern and Southern states?
    a) Labour Day
    b) Thanksgiving Day
    c) New Year's Day
    d) Independence Day

235. What is the only temperature that is same on both the Celsius and Fahrenheit scales?
    a) -50 degrees
    b) -40 degrees
    c) -20 degrees
    d) -10 degrees

236. The world's busiest airports by passenger traffic are measured by total passengers (data from Airports Council International (ACI)), defined as passengers enplaned plus passengers deplaned plus direct-transit passengers. Which of the following tops the list?
    a) London Heathrow Airport
    b) Beijing Capital International Airport
    c) Hartsfield–Jackson Atlanta International Airport
    d) Frankfurt Airport

237. The first ever Afro-Asian games were held in which city?
   a) Cape Town   b) Hyderabad
   c) Lahore   d) Beijing

238. The birth name of which Mughal emperor was Nur-ud-din which means, 'Light of the Faith'?
   a) Akbar   b) Jahangir
   c) Shah Jahan   d) Humayun

239. The Axis powers were the nations that fought in the Second World War against the Allied forces. Which of the following nations was not an Axis power?
   a) Japan   b) Germany
   c) Italy   d) China

240. The Ramon Magsaysay awards are named after the President of which country?
   a) Philippines b) Vietnam
   c) Indonesia   d) Japan

241. What is the name of the newspaper that *Spiderman's* alias Peter Parker works for?
   a) The Daily Planet   b) The Daily Bugle
   c) The Daily Herald   d) The Daily Venus

242. A notable ornithologist, A. O. Hume has been called 'The Father of Indian Ornithology'. He is known for founding which famous organisation?
   a) Indian National Congress   b) Red Cross
   c) World Wildlife Fund   d) United Nations

243. Which city was established by Dost Mohammad Khan, an Afghan soldier in the Mughal army? The city is known as the *City of Lakes* for its various *natural* as well as *artificial lakes*.
   a) Mysore   b) Shimla

Multiple Choice Questions

c) Bhopal   d) Haridwar

244. Which adventure novel was first published as a book on May 23, 1883? It was originally serialised in the children's magazine, *Young Folks* between 1881 and 1882 under the title 'The mutiny of the Hispaniola' with Stevenson adopting the pseudonym, Captain George North.

   a) *Treasure Island*   b) *Moby Dick*
   c) *A Tale of Two Cities*   d) *Jane Eyre*

245. Which of these football players belong to France?

   a) Pele   b) David Beckham
   c) Ronaldinho   d) Zinadine Zidane

246. *Operation Polo* was a military operation in September 1948 in which the *Indian Armed Forces* invaded this state and overthrew its Nizam, annexing the state into the Indian Union. Identify the state.

   a) Bangalore (Bengaluru)   b) Hyderabad
   c) Chennai   d) Pondicherry

247. Before the devastating floods of 1937, Sir M. Visveswararya proposed a detailed investigation for storage reservoirs in the Mahanadi basin to tackle the problem of floods in the Mahanadi delta that resulted in the development of which dam?

   a) Hirakud Dam   b) Bhakra Dam
   c) Tehri Dam   d) Tungabhadra dam

248. Which element occurs in deposits throughout the world mostly as cinnabar?

   a) Tungsten   b) Mercury
   c) Hydrogen   d) Carbon

249. *Guru Purnima* is a Hindu festival dedicated to spiritual and academic teachers. It is celebrated in the honour of which great sage?

   a) Agastya   b) Atreya
   c) Vashistha   d) Vyasa

250. Which Bollywood actor started his career in a Military Censor Office with a salary of Rs. 165?
   a) Dev Anand   b) Ashok Kumar
   c) Dilip Kumar   d) Amitabh Bachchan

251. Name the largest Muslim country that is home to 12.7% of the world's Muslims.
   a) Indonesia   b) Afghanistan
   c) Pakistan   d) Bangladesh

252. A *cataract* is a clouding of which part inside the eye which leads to a decrease in vision?
   a) Cornea   b) Pupil
   c) Lens   d) Iris

253. The name of which country comes from a tree that once grew plentifully along the coast of this country?
   a) Zaire   b) Brazil
   c) Zimbabwe   d) Germany

254. Who was the founding director of two well-known research institutions, namely the *Tata Institute of Fundamental Research* (TIFR) and the *Trombay Atomic Energy Establishment*?
   a) Homi Bhabha   b) C.V. Raman
   c) P.C. Ray   d) Salim Ali

255. Evangelista Torricelli was an Italian physicist and mathematician, best known for his invention of which scientific instrument used in meteorology?
   a) Voltameter   b) Barometer
   c) Ammeter   d) Oscilloscope

256. Name the prefix that denotes a factor of ten in the metric system.
   a) Mega   b) Giga
   c) Tera   d) Deca

257. The name of which character from the *Mahabharata* implies that he was not gestated in a womb, but outside the human body in a vessel or a basket.

Multiple Choice Questions

a) Bhishma b) Drona
c) Arjun d) Vyasa

258. Upon taking power in 1959, Castro banned all sets of which popular game?

   a) Ludo b) Snakes and Ladders
   c) Monopoly d) Scrabble

259. Which city is widely known as the 'Windy City', although Milton (Massachusetts) is the windiest city in the United States?

   a) Chicago b) New York
   c) Los Angeles d) Houston

260. Annika Sörenstam is a retired Swedish professional in which sport?

   a) Badminton b) Tennis
   c) Cricket d) Golf

261. Who is referred to as the 'Black Pimpernel' in the press? It is a reference to Emma Orczy's 1905 novel *The Scarlet Pimpernel*.

   a) Nelson Mandela b) Barack Obama
   c) Muhammad Ali d) Jesse Owens

262. In 1933, who left IACS to join the Indian Institute of Science in Bengaluru as its first Indian director?

   a) Swami Vivekananda b) C.V. Raman
   c) P. C. Ray d) J.C. Bose

263. Who was created as a replacement for Oswald the Lucky Rabbit, an earlier cartoon character created by the Disney studio for Charles Mintz, a film producer who distributed product through Universal Studios? He officially debuted in the short film, *Steamboat Willie* (1928).

   a) Donald Duck b) Goofy
   c) Popeye d) Mickey Mouse

264. Which of the following cities is known as the *City of Mosques*, and with 400,000 cycle-rickshaws running on its streets every day, the city is described as the *Rickshaw Capital of the World*?

a) Dhaka b) New Delhi
c) Lahore d) Kathmandu

265. The name of which Indian state literally means, 'land of the hill people'?
   a) Mizoram b) Arunachal Pradesh
   c) Meghalaya d) Manipur

266. Who amongst the following is the first US President to have been born in Hawaii?
   a) Bill Clinton b) Bill Gates
   c) Barack Obama d) George Washington

267. In 1983, Parle came out with the 'Goldspotting' campaign in its tie-up with this Walt Disney film in India. Which one?
   a) Popeye b) Winnie the Pooh
   c) Jungle Book d) Mickey Mouse

268. Which book published in 1859 is the largest selling single volume book ever? It sold 2 million copies till date.
   a) *Gitanjali* b) *David Copperfield*
   c) *Othello* d) *A Tale of Two Cities*

269. Gmail, as we know was earlier derived from another free service named after a cartoon character. Which one?
   a) Garfield b) Goofy
   c) Donald Duck d) Popeye

270. Whose autobiography is titled 'Freedom in Exile'?
   a) Nelson Mandela b) Dalai Lama
   c) Barack Obama d) Mahatma Gandhi

271. The former name, *Formosa* of which state in East Asia dates from 1544, when the Portuguese sailors sighted this island and named it *Ilha Formosa*, which means, 'Beautiful Island'?
   a) China b) Taiwan
   c) Singapore d) Hong Kong

272. What type of reference book did Samuel Johnson write in the middle of the 18th century?

a) Encyclopedia b) Pictionary
c) Atlas d) Dictionary

273. The present-day Mongolians regard him as the *founding father of Mongolia*. Who is he?
   a) Fa Hien b) Hiuen Tsang
   c) Genghis Khan d) Chanakya

274. Samuel Langhorne Clemens was an American author and humorist. Identify his pen name.
   a) Louis Stevenson b) Mark Twain
   c) Thomas Hardy d) P.G. Wodehouse

275. Daniel Gabriel Fahrenheit was a physicist, engineer and a glass blower who is best known for inventing what?
   a) Stethoscope b) Mercury Thermometer
   c) Syringe d) Crocin

276. *Moonwalk* is an autobiography written by which American musician?
   a) Elvis Presley b) Eric Clapton
   c) Bob Dylan d) Michael Jackson

277. He was a French military engineer and physicist, often described as the 'father of thermodynamics'. In his only publication, the 1824 monograph, *Reflections* on the *Motive Power of Fire*, he gave the first successful theory of the maximum efficiency of heat engines. Identify him.
   a) Lord Kelvin b) Marie Curie
   c) Louis Pasteur d) Nicolas Carnot

278. Which actor was born as Harihar Jethalal Zariwala in 1938 to a Gujarati Jain family and spent his early years in Surat?
   a) Kishore Kumar b) Ashok Kumar
   c) Raj Kumar d) Sanjeev Kumar

279. Who lives under the name, Mr. Sanders in a house located in the Hundred Acre Wood?

a) Popeye b) Donald Duck
c) Winnie-the-Pooh d) Mickey Mouse

280. Following is a quote from which famous book?

"It was the best of times, it was the worst of times, it was the age of wisdom, it was the age of foolishness, it was the epoch of belief, it was the epoch of incredulity, it was the season of light, it was the season of darkness, it was the spring of hope, it was the winter of despair…"

a) Great Expectations b) Othello
c) A Tale of Two Cities d) Jane Eyre

281. Which Austrian composer who died in 1791 aged only 35 had the forenames, *Wolfgang Amadeus*?

a) Mozart b) Beethoven
c) Franz Schubert d) Joseph Haydn

282. The name of which religion means, 'disciple' in Hindi?

a) Sikhism b) Hinduism
c) Buddhism d) Christianity

283. Which self-governing island is known as *Kalaallit Nunaat* in the language of its indigenous people?

a) Ireland b) Iceland
c) New Zealand d) Greenland

284. Which of Shakespeare's tragic heroes speaks the words, 'To be or not to be, that is the question'?

a) Ben Hur b) Romeo
c) Macbeth d) Hamlet

285. This is a quote from which famous book?
"All animals are equal, but some animals are more equal than others."

a) Animal Farm b) Jungle Book
c) Great Expectations d) Oliver Twist

Multiple Choice Questions

286. Romano Prodi and Silvio Berlusconi are two recent Prime Ministers of which European country?
   a) Rome
   b) Venice
   c) France
   d) Italy

287. The Tanjore painting is a major form of classical South Indian painting from which Indian state?
   a) Andhra Pradesh
   b) Karnataka
   c) Tamil Nadu
   d) Kerala

288. Which city is located on the right bank of the river, Sarayu, 6 km from Faizabad? The city is 9,000 years old, and was founded by *Manu*, the first *man in the Vedas*, and *law-giver of the Hindus*.
   a) Pataliputra
   b) Taxila
   c) Ayodhya
   d) Kurukshetra

289. In the *First Battle of Panipat in 1526*, the Mughal forces of Babur defeated the much larger ruling army of which Sultan of Delhi?
   a) Ibrahim Lodi
   b) Akbar
   c) Jahangir
   d) Humayun

290. The Osmania University is a state university established and named after Mir Osman Ali Khan. It is the first Indian university to have Urdu as a medium of instruction. In which state is it located?
   a) Bengaluru
   b) Chennai
   c) Lucknow
   d) Hyderabad

291. There is an inscription above the entryway to Wimbledon Centre Court which reads, 'If you can meet with triumph and disaster/and treat those two imposters just the same' – are the lines of a famous poem. Who is the poet?
   a) William Shakespeare
   b) Rudyard Kipling

c) John Keats   d) Rabindranath Tagore

292. Sivakasi is a town in Virudhunagar District in which Indian state? The town is known for fire-crackers and match factories that produce 70 percent of the country's produce. The printing industries in Sivakasi produce 30 percent of the total diaries produced in India.

   a) Tamil Nadu   b) Karnataka
   c) Kerala   d) Maharashtra

293. The *House of Orange* is a princely dynasty that derived its name from the medieval principality of Orange, in old Province in southern France. The dynasty is the royal family of which country?

   a) Australia   b) New Zealand
   c) Netherlands   d) Ethiopia

294. Which epic novel written by professor J. R. R. Tolkien began as a sequel to his 1937 children's fantasy novel, *The Hobbit*, but eventually, developed into a much larger work?

   a) *The Lord of the Rings*   b) *Avatar*
   c) *Terminator*   d) *Gladiator*

295. Who is the main villain of the book, *Animal Farm* written by George Orwell?

   a) Napoleon   b) Bismarck
   c) Fa-Hien   d) Hitler

296. *The Velvet Revolution* was a non-violent transition of power in which country? The effect of the revolution was the end of the *41 years of Communist rule* and peaceful dissolution of the nation into two countries.

   a) Yugosalvia   b) Romania
   c) Germany   d) Czechoslovakia

297. Who made his first film, *Through the Eyes of a Painter* in 1967?

Multiple Choice Questions

    a) Amrita Pritam   b) M.F. Husain
    c) Satish Gujral   d) Tyeb Mehta

298. The lead heroine charged Rs. 11/- and the person on whom the story was based on, charged Rs. 1/-. Which 2013 film was this?

    a) *Bhaag Milkha Bhaag*   b) *Satyagraha*
    c) *Chennai Express*   d) *Saheb, Biwi Aur Gangster Returns*

299. When this country seceded from the Netherlands, many battles between European powers were fought in the area of this country, causing it to be dubbed the 'Battlefield of Europe,' a reputation strengthened by both World Wars. Identify.

    a) Belgium   b) Ukraine
    c) Germany   d) Austria

300. Who composed the music and sang for two dance sequences in the Satyajit Ray's *Shatranj ke Khiladi*, and choreographed the song, *Kaahe Chhed Mohe* from the 2002 film version of *Devdas*?

    a) Saroj Khan   b) Birju Maharaj
    c) Mallika Sarabhai   d) Shiamak Davar

Answers

1. Harappa
2. Arvind Adiga
3. Boxing
4. Stephen Hawking
5. Mt. Vesuvius
6. Heart
7. Saunf
8. Netaji Subhash Chandra Bose
9. Swimming
10. Apple
11. Invention of instant noodles
12. Karna
13. Karachi
14. Ratan Tata
15. Allahabad
16. Aamir Khan
17. Bengaluru
18. Microsoft
19. Basketball
20. Meerut
21. Sodium
22. Matrix
23. Bangladesh
24. Sher Shah Suri
25. Red Fort
26. Jahangir
27. Arya Samaj
28. Lord Curzon
29. Valmiki
30. Konark Sun Temple
31. Shani
32. Parsis
33. Khalsa
34. Brahma
35. Taxila
36. Pokharan
37. Jawaharlal Nehru
38. Swami Vivekanand
39. Arjun Singh
40. Folketin
41. Mayawati
42. Sachin Pilot
43. SAARC
44. Hillary Clinton
45. Rashtrapati Bhavan
46. France
47. Vice President of India
48. Bill Clinton

49.	Kalyan Singh	77.	Sivaji The Boss
50.	Morarji Desai, Indira Gandhi	78.	AlyquePadamsee
51.	Benazir Bhutto	79.	Mumbai Beat
52.	Pervez Musharraf	80.	Hyderabad
53.	Richard Nixon	81.	Verve
54.	Cardamom	82.	Satyam Shivam Sundaram
55.	Frappe	83.	Homeopathy
56.	Hilsa	84.	Potassium
57.	Gulab Jamub	85.	Sulphur
58.	Risotto	86.	X-Rays
59.	McDonald's	87.	Refraction
60.	À la carte	88.	Formalin
61.	Sushi	89.	Concave Mirror
62.	Sanjeev Kapoor	90.	Hydrogen Sulphide
63.	Tandoori Chicken	91.	Acetone
64.	Clove	92.	Farad
65.	Barista	93.	Dhanvantari
66.	Pizza	94.	Galileo Galilei
67.	Tarla Dalal	95.	Gall Bladder
68.	Farhan Akhtar	96.	Nikola Tesla
69.	Nutan	97.	Solitaire
70.	Slumdog Millionaire	98.	Basketball
71.	Backstreet Boys	99.	Table Tennis
72.	Titanic	100.	10 feet
73.	AYS	101.	Table Tennis
74.	Karan Johar	102.	ESPN
75.	Daniel Craig	103.	Diego Maradona
76.	Ricky Martin	104.	Olympics

105. Basketball
106. Snakes & Ladder
107. Harsha Bhogle
108. Lala Amarnath
109. Rajyavardhan Singh Rathore
110. Danny Boyle
111. Appu
112. Facebook
113. Java
114. Cybernaut
115. Apple Computers
116. Sabeer Bhatia
117. Moore's Law
118. Biometrics
119. Integrated Circuits
120. NFS
121. COMPAQ
122. Nandan Nilekani
123. Azim Premji
124. IBM
125. Beta
126. Bhuvan
127. Peso
128. Bangkok
129. Bahadur Shah Zafar
130. Spain
131. Kulkarni
132. League of Nations
133. Mumbai
134. Shiv Sena
135. Kalidas
136. Gujarati
137. Tatas
138. Muslim League
139. Renuka Shahane
140. Binaca
141. Friends
142. 080
143. Mysore
144. Enid Blyton
145. 17
146. Pongal
147. Linkin Park
148. Batman
149. Himachal Pradesh
150. Rock Street Journal
151. Stuttgart
152. Buddha
153. Dubai
154. Hum Log
155. Tide
156. Ernest Hemmingway
157. Reita Faria
158. Charles Babbage
159. Muhammad Yunus

Multiple Choice Questions

160. Paintball
161. The Rolling Stones
162. Gulzarilal Nanda
163. Woodrow Wilson
164. Jazz
165. Narayan Murthy
166. Marco Polo
167. BCCI
168. Indian Ocean
169. Mahatma Gandhi
170. Zaheer Abbas
171. Gateway of India
172. Donald Duck
173. Gwalior
174. Raman Effect
175. Indra
176. Champaner
177. Punjab
178. Nutan
179. Tripura
180. Maharaja Ranjit Singh
181. Euclid
182. Red Fort
183. Taxila
184. Hurricane
185. Kolkata
186. Parashurama
187. Rani Lakshmi Bai
188. Hema Malini
189. Freon
190. Rajendra Prasad
191. Baseball
192. LokmanyaTilak
193. Stafford Cripps
194. Japan
195. Barack Obama
196. King Kong
197. Surat
198. Arsenal
199. Premchand
200. Finland
201. Rajendra Prasad
202. Leonardo da Vinci
203. David Headley
204. Dr. Hargobind Khorana
205. Jatayu
206. Andhra Pradesh
207. Isaac Newton
208. Mexican
209. Femur
210. Khajuraho
211. Adolf Hitler
212. Badminton
213. 7
214. VirendraSehwag
215. Ujjain

216. Syed Kirmani
217. Balarama
218. Robert Frost
219. Kuchipudi
220. JK Rowling
221. Morarji Desai
222. Krypton
223. Muhammad Bin Tughlaq
224. Bal Gangadhar Tilak
225. Major Radcliffe
226. Hawaii
227. Gujarat
228. New York
229. Angel Falls
230. Spain
231. Broadway
232. Levi Strauss
233. Berlin
234. Thanksgiving Day
235. -40 degrees
236. Hartsfield–Jackson Atlanta International Airport
237. Hyderabad
238. Jahangir
239. China
240. Phillippines
241. The Daily Bugle
242. Indian National Congress
243. Bhopal
244. Treasure Island
245. Zinadine Zidane
246. Hyderabad
247. Hirakud Dam
248. Mercury
249. Vyasa
250. DevAnand
251. Indonesia
252. Lens
253. Brazil
254. Homi Bhabha
255. Barometer
256. Deca
257. Drona
258. Monopoly
259. Chicago
260. Golf
261. Nelson Mandela
262. C.V. Raman
263. Mickey Mouse
264. Dhaka
265. Mizoram
266. Barack Obama
267. Jungle Book
268. A Tale of Two Cities
269. Garfield
270. Nelson Mandela

Multiple Choice Questions

271. Taiwan
272. Dictionary
273. Genghis Khan
274. Mark Twain
275. Mercury Thermometer
276. Michael Jackson
277. Nicolas Carnot
278. Sanjeev Kumar
279. Winnie-the-Pooh
280. A Tale of Two Cities
281. Mozart
282. Sikhism
283. Greenland
284. Hamlet
285. Animal Farm
286. Italy
287. Karnataka
288. Ayodhya
289. Ibrahim Lodi
290. Hyderabad
291. Rudyard Kipling
292. Tamil Nadu
293. Netherlands
294. The Lord of the Rings
295. Napoleon
296. Czechoslovakia
297. M.F. Husain
298. Bhaag Milkha Bhaag
299. Belgium
300. Birju Maharaj

www.ingramcontent.com/pod-product-compliance
Lightning Source LLC
Chambersburg PA
CBHW070333230426
43663CB00011B/2297